THE SCOTTISH ENLIGHTENMENT

2010 DIARY

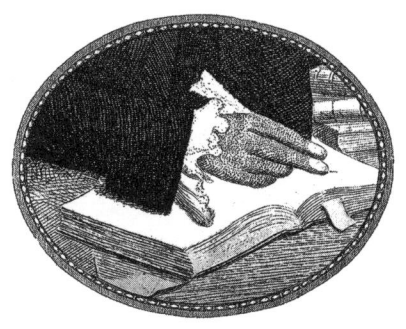

WITH ENGRAVINGS BY

JOHN KAY

1742–1826

BIRLINN

Published in 2009 by
Birlinn Limited
West Newington House
10 Newington Road
Edinburgh
EH9 1QS

www.birlinn.co.uk

ISBN 978 1 84158 731 8

Designed and Typeset in Adobe Jenson
by Joe Szatkowski

Printed and bound in Slovenia

couthie

From his print shop window, John Kay (1742–1826), the Edinburgh-based barber, miniature painter and social commentator, was able to observe at first hand many of the characters of the Scottish Enlightenment. It was a golden age that saw remarkable changes in law, philosophy, science, literature, the arts, engineering and architecture. James Hutton and Joseph Black along with Adam Smith, William Cullen and Hugh Blair were all subjects for Kay's burin and his engravings offer a unique record of the multifaceted yet relatively couthie society of a post-1707 'republic of letters' in Scotland.

Scholars continue to debate the exact dates and impact of the Scottish Enlightenment, but most agree that at its hub were the urban intelligentsia of the universities of Aberdeen, Edinburgh and Glasgow. The many clubs and societies that flourished in the eighteenth century and the publishing houses, especially in Edinburgh, also played a key role in the dissemination of new ideas amongst a diverse audience, as did the growing number of magazines, journals, pamphlets and diaries.

John Letts launched the first commercial diary in 1812 in response to merchants' needs. Much refined, the basic form and utility persists to this day. *The Scottish Enlightenment 2010 Diary* aims to highlight the diverse events, activities and characters – influencers, participants and heirs – of an exceptional period in Scottish history. The word 'diary' derives from the Latin, *diarium* meaning 'daily allowance'. In keeping with this original sense, the quotations and historical events cited are brief and largely contemporary with Kay's lifetime. Consequently, each of these diary entries serves up an *amuse-gueule* from a magnificent platter of achievement and philosophical thought.

SHEILA SZATKOWSKI
Editor

PHILOSOPHERS

Philosophers (1787) Dr James Hutton and Dr Joseph Black in conversation, their sonsie faces 'full of science'.

ARCHIBALD CONSTABLE ESQ.
BOOKSELLER.

Archibald Constable, Esq., Bookseller (1823)

This etching of the famous bookseller and 'Prince of Publishers' appears in the 1877 edition of Kay's Portraits.

Lord Kames, Hugo Arnot of Balcormo, Advocate, Lord Monboddo (1784)

CONNOISSEURS

Connoisseurs (1785)

William Scott, on the left, peers through his glass at a print held by James Sibbald, while opposite, George Fairholme clutches a portait of 'the grinning auctioneer.' James Kerr and a bespectacled man both look on. The figure on the far right may be Kay himself.

Ioannes Bruno M.D.
Hercule! Opium minime sedat

Dr Brown in his study (1791)

Dr John Brown was a close associate of Dr William Cullen up until he published his Brunonian System of Medicine in *Elementa Medicinae* (1780) which contradicted Cullen's own medical theories and caused much controversy for several years after his death in 1788.

(opposite) **Dr Cullen in his study (1787)**

William Cullen moved from the University of Glasgow in 1755 to take up the Chair of Chemistry and Medicine at Edinburgh and was a key figure in making Edinburgh one of the great centres for medical education in Europe.

(middle) **Rev. Hugh Blair, D.D. of the High Church, Edinburgh (1798)**

Blair is best known for his *Sermons* and *Lectures on Rhetoric and Belles Lettres*. He was an admirer of the works of Robert Burns and promoted the authenticity of the Poems of Ossian.

(lower) **Rev. John Jamieson, D.D. (1799)**

Born in Glasgow, Jamieson compiled the *Etymological Dictionary of the Scottish Language* (1808).

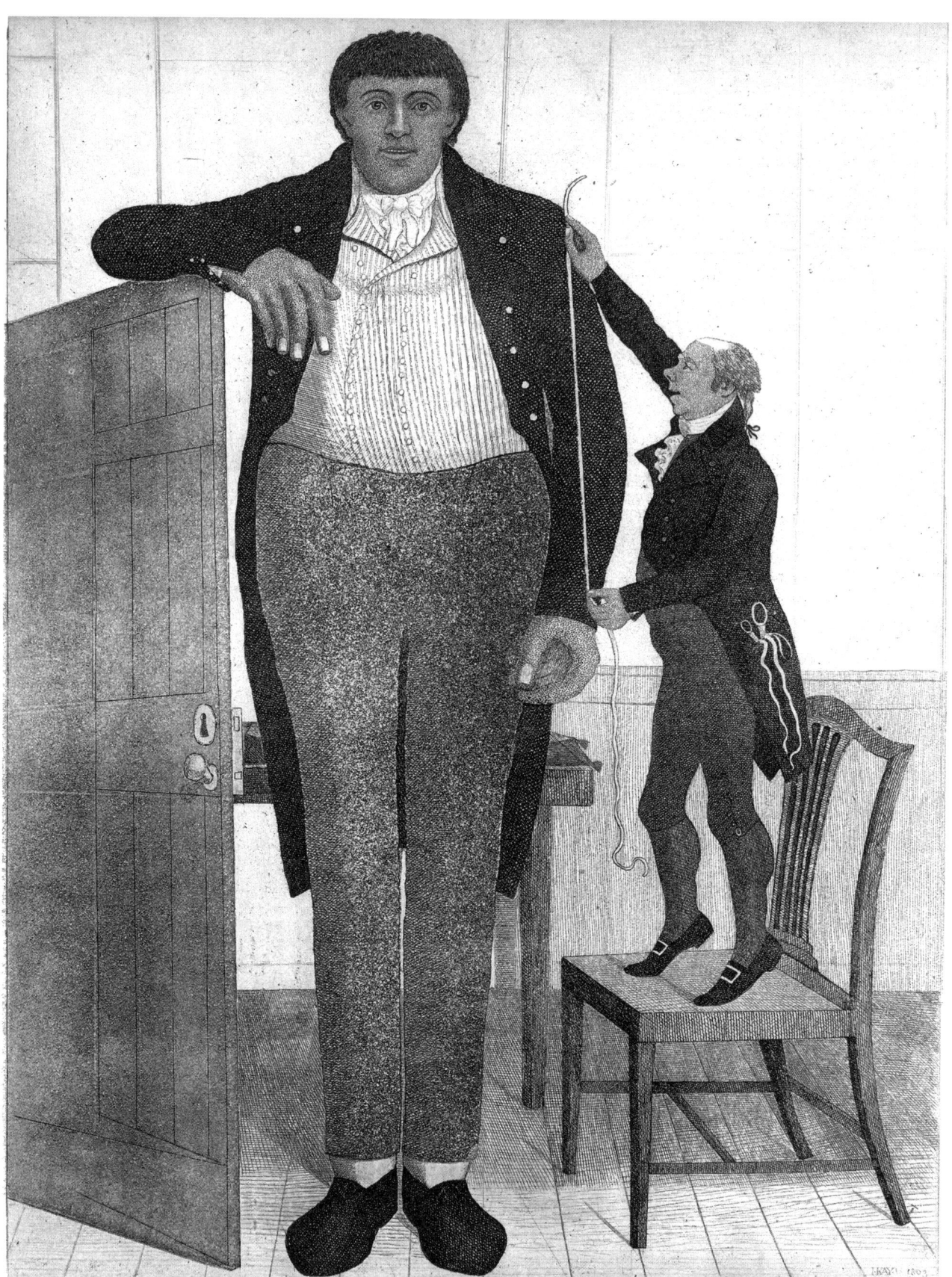

Travells Eldest Son in Conversation with a Cherokee Chief.

How dare you approach me with your travells. There is not a single word of them true.
There you may be right, and altho I never dined upon the Lion or eat half a Cow and turned
the rest to grafs, yet my works have been of more use to mankind than yours
and there is more truth in one page of my Edin.ʳ direptory than in all your five
Volumes 4º. So when you talk to me dont imagine yourself at the Source of the Nile!

I. Kay Del. et Sculp.ᵗ Publifhed as the Act Directs 1791

Two travellers: James Bruce Esq. of Kinnaird, and Peter Williamson (1791)
Bruce, the Abyssinian traveller, raggles with 'Indian' Peter, publisher of the first Edinburgh
Street Directory.

(*opposite*) **O'Brien, the Irish giant, and William Ranken, Esq. (1803)**
The scene is an imaginary depiction of the giant being measured for a greatcoat.

(left) **Dr William Robertson, D.D., in his full clerical dress (1790)**
William Robertson, Historiographer for Scotland, was Principal of Edinburgh University from 1761 until his death in 1793.

(right) **Alexander Carlyle, D.D., Inveresk (1789)**
Minister at Inveresk for 57 years, the Reverend Carlyle, known as 'Jupiter' on account of his striking physique, was a leader of the moderates in the church and a close associate of Principal William Robertson and John Home, the dramatist.

Twelve Advocates Who Plead Without Wigs (1811)

Adam Gillies	Alexander Irving	James Millar
Sir Walter Scott	Robert Corbet	George Joseph Bell
William Rose Robinson	John Wright	John Graham Dalyell
Francis Jeffrey	John Jardine	John Cunninghame

I Say we are fearfully & wonderfully made

Alexander Hunter Esq. of Polmood, and Roger Hog, Esq. of Newliston (n.d.)

Alexander Hunter was a well-known wealthy merchant in Edinburgh. Roger Hog, a corpulent merchant who had made his fortune in London, prefaced every sentence with, "I say," a mannerism picked up by Kay, who also refers to the biblical words in Psalm 139:14: "I will praise you, for I am fearfully and wonderfully made; marvellous are your works, and that my soul knows very well."

MODERN NURSING

Modern Nursing (1796)

18th-century society ladies embraced Jean-Jacques Rousseau's call to return to nature by breastfeeding their own children. The challenge for dressmakers was to bring fashion and function together. Kay's print was published in the same year as James Gillray's satirical *The Fashionable Mama or The Convenience of Modern Dress*.

The Sapient Septemviri

1 *The Beauty of Holiness, Lecturing.*

2 *Had you not sold your Patronages, First Minister might have been annexed to my Divine Chair of Verity & taste.*

3 *Annually for 45 years and upwards have I beat up, even to the Ultima Thule have I recruited our University.*

4 *I have rendered Vernacular the Greek Language from Aberdour to Aberdeen.*

5 *Agriculture is the Noblest of Sciences, mind your Glebes, the Emperor of China is a Farmer.*

6 *Has not the Effulgence of my Countenance been a light unto your feet, and a lamp unto your Paths.*

7 *Colledge property, Patronages are unalienable, so says the Law, the Noble Patron has rewarded most justly your Rapacity*

8 *Degrees Male and Female in Medicine and Midwifery, sold here for ready money.*

The Sapient Septemviri, King's College, Aberdeen (1786)

The Sapient Septemviri or 'seven wise men' of King's College caricatured in Kay's print objected to a plan prepared in 1786 for uniting King's and Marischal Colleges.

1. Dr Skene Ogilvy inculcating on the Septemviri the duty of returning good for evil.

2. Dr Alexander Gerard, Professor of Divinity, author of works on Taste and Genius.

3. Mr Roderick M'Leod, Sub-Principal, and ardent recruiter of Highland students.

4. John Leslie, Professor of Greek, and friend of the historian William Robertson.

5. Dr John Chalmers, Principal of King's College for almost 30 years.

6. Thomas Gordon, Professor of Philosophy, known as 'humorist Gordon'.

7. Dr William Thom, Professor of Civil Law.

8. Dr William Chalmers, Professor of Medicine.

(*opposite*) **Mr Clinch and Mrs Yates in the characters of the Duke and Duchess of Braganza (1785)**
None of the surrounding faces has been identified.

(*lower*) **A Group of Aeronauts, 'Fowls of A Feather Flock Together' (1785)**
Vincent Lunardi is the central figure, reaching out to greet James 'Balloon' Tytler.

Duke and Duchess of Braganza

Fowls of a Feather Flock together.

Year Calendar 2010

January
M	T	W	T	F	S	S
				1	2	3
4	5	6	7	8	9	10
11	12	13	14	15	16	17
18	19	20	21	22	23	24
25	26	27	28	29	30	31

February
M	T	W	T	F	S	S
1	2	3	4	5	6	7
8	9	10	11	12	13	14
15	16	17	18	19	20	21
22	23	24	25	26	27	28

March
M	T	W	T	F	S	S
1	2	3	4	5	6	7
8	9	10	11	12	13	14
15	16	17	18	19	20	21
22	23	24	25	26	27	28
29	30	31				

April
M	T	W	T	F	S	S
			1	2	3	4
5	6	7	8	9	10	11
12	13	14	15	16	17	18
19	20	21	22	23	24	25
26	27	28	29	30		

May
M	T	W	T	F	S	S
					1	2
3	4	5	6	7	8	9
10	11	12	13	14	15	16
17	18	19	20	21	22	23
24	25	26	27	28	29	30
31						

June
M	T	W	T	F	S	S
	1	2	3	4	5	6
7	8	9	10	11	12	13
14	15	16	17	18	19	20
21	22	23	24	25	26	27
28	29	30				

July
M	T	W	T	F	S	S
			1	2	3	4
5	6	7	8	9	10
11	12	13	14	15	16	17
18	19	20	21	22	23	24
25	26	27	28	29	30	31

August
M	T	W	T	F	S	S
						1
2	3	4	5	6	7	8
9	10	11	12	13	14	15
16	17	18	19	20	21	22
23	24	25	26	27	28	29
30	31					

September
M	T	W	T	F	S	S
		1	2	3	4	5
6	7	8	9	10	11	12
13	14	15	16	17	18	19
20	21	22	23	24	25	26
27	28	29	30			

October
M	T	W	T	F	S	S
				1	2	3
4	5	6	7	8	9	10
11	12	13	14	15	16	17
18	19	20	21	22	23	24
25	26	27	28	29	30	31

November
M	T	W	T	F	S	S
1	2	3	4	5	6	7
8	9	10	11	12	13	14
15	16	17	18	19	20	21
22	23	24	25	26	27	28
29	30					

December
M	T	W	T	F	S	S
		1	2	3	4	5
6	7	8	9	10	11	12
13	14	15	16	17	18	19
20	21	22	23	24	25	26
27	28	29	30	31		

Year Calendar 2011

January
M	T	W	T	F	S	S
					1	2
3	4	5	6	7	8	9
10	11	12	13	14	15	16
17	18	19	20	21	22	23
24	25	26	27	28	29	30
31						

February
M	T	W	T	F	S	S
	1	2	3	4	5	6
7	8	9	10	11	12	13
14	15	16	17	18	19	20
21	22	23	24	25	26	27
28						

March
M	T	W	T	F	S	S
	1	2	3	4	5	6
7	8	9	10	11	12	13
14	15	16	17	18	19	20
21	22	23	24	25	26	27
28	29	30	31			

April
M	T	W	T	F	S	S
				1	2	3
4	5	6	7	8	9	10
11	12	13	14	15	16	17
18	19	20	21	22	23	24
25	26	27	28	29	30	

May
M	T	W	T	F	S	S
						1
2	3	4	5	6	7	8
9	10	11	12	13	14	15
16	17	18	19	20	21	22
23	24	25	26	27	28	29
30	31					

June
M	T	W	T	F	S	S
		1	2	3	4	5
6	7	8	9	10	11	12
13	14	15	16	17	18	19
20	21	22	23	24	25	26
27	28	29	30			

July
M	T	W	T	F	S	S
				1	2	3
4	5	6	7	8	9	10
11	12	13	14	15	16	17
18	19	20	21	22	23	24
25	26	27	28	29	30	31

August
M	T	W	T	F	S	S
1	2	3	4	5	6	7
8	9	10	11	12	13	14
15	16	17	18	19	20	21
22	23	24	25	26	27	28
29	30	31				

September
M	T	W	T	F	S	S
			1	2	3	4
5	6	7	8	9	10	11
12	13	14	15	16	17	18
19	20	21	22	23	24	25
26	27	28	29	30		

October
M	T	W	T	F	S	S
					1	2
3	4	5	6	7	8	9
10	11	12	13	14	15	16
17	18	19	20	21	22	23
24	25	26	27	28	29	30
31						

November
M	T	W	T	F	S	S
	1	2	3	4	5	6
7	8	9	10	11	12	13
14	15	16	17	18	19	20
21	22	23	24	25	26	27
28	29	30				

December
M	T	W	T	F	S	S
			1	2	3	4
5	6	7	8	9	10	11
12	13	14	15	16	17	18
19	20	21	22	23	24	25
26	27	28	29	30	31	

Dr James Hutton liked a sound sleep and used to say "a good bed was the best of all situations for a philosopher". *The Anecdotes and Egotisms of Henry Mackenzie* (1927)

"Society may be formed so as to exist without crime, without poverty, with health greatly improved, with little, if any misery, and with intelligence and happiness increased a hundredfold; and no obstacle whatsoever intervenes at this moment except ignorance to prevent such a state of society from becoming universal." Robert Owen in *An Address to the Inhabitants of New Lanark* (1816)

1780 Jedburgh's famous daughter, the mathematician Mary Somerville, was born. Her protective father once expressed concern that "the strain of abstract thought" would injure her "tender female frame".

1800 Hugh Blair (b.1718), Professor of Rhetoric and Belles Lettres at Edinburgh, famous for his *Sermons* and praise for the *Poems of Ossian*, died in Edinburgh and was buried in Greyfriars.

December 2009

28 MONDAY
Public Holiday
(UK, IRL, AUS & CAN)

"Between a couple of young advocates sits a decent grocer from Bristo Street, and amidst a host of shop-lads ... is perched a stiffish young probationer who ... has much dread that the company will sit late." Robert Chambers, describing the lively tavern society in the Old Town of Edinburgh

29 TUESDAY

1747 *The Aberdeen Journal* was first published, later to become *The Press and Journal.*

30 WEDNESDAY

1797 David Martin (b.1737), Scots artist and engraver, died in Edinburgh. His portrait of Benjamin Franklin hangs in the White House in Washington DC.

THURSDAY *31*

"For a long course of years his shop, during a part of the day, was the resort of most of the clergy of the city, of the professors of the University, and other public men and eminent authors; and his dwelling-house was equally frequented in the morning hours by many of the same characters, who met to discuss with him their literary projects." Dugald Stewart recollecting the publisher, William Creech

FRIDAY *1*
New Year's Day

1766 James Stewart, the Old Pretender, died in Rome. He was buried in St Peter's Basilica in the Vatican. His sons, Charles Edward and Henry Benedict Stuart, are also buried in the Vatican.

SATURDAY *2*

1818 The inaugural meeting of the Institution of Civil Engineers, of which Thomas Telford was first president, took place at the Kendal Coffee House in Fleet Street, London.

SUNDAY *3*

1814 It was a night of good cheer as Sir John Marjoribanks assembled 100 guests at his home to celebrate Walter Scott and the 9th Earl of Dalhousie receiving the Freedom of the City of Edinburgh.

January 2010

4 MONDAY
Public Holiday (SCO)

1775 According to the historian Hugo Arnot, the duty paid for wine imported at Leith over the last twelve months had been £25,277 12s 6d, almost double the sum paid in the previous year.

5 TUESDAY

"As taste gives the last finishing to genius in the author or performer, so it is the fundamental ingredient in the character of the critic." Alexander Gerard, *An Essay on Taste* (1759)

6 WEDNESDAY

1730 The author of *The Rudiments of the Latin Tongue*, Thomas Ruddiman, was appointed Keeper of the Advocates' Library in Edinburgh.

THURSDAY 7

1758 The key figure in the revival of Scots vernacular poetry, Allan Ramsay (b.1686), died of scurvy at his home at Castlehill in Edinburgh. Wigmaker, bookseller and poet, he was author of *The Gentle Shepherd*.

FRIDAY 8

"You have great advantages in going to study at Edinburgh at the time when there happens to be collected a set of truly great men, professors of the several branches of knowledge, as have ever appeared in an Age or Country". Benjamin Franklin in a letter to Jonathan Potts (1776)

SATURDAY 9

"Persons of good sense ... seldom fall into argument, except lawyers, university men, and men of all sorts that have been bred in Edinburgh." Benjamin Franklin

SUNDAY 10

1752 The first meeting of the Literary Society of Glasgow brought together savants such as William Cullen and Adam Smith and was to act as a sounding board for works such as *The Wealth of Nations*.

January 2010

11 MONDAY

"In Edinburgh, the access to men of parts is not only easy, but their conversation and the communication of their knowledge are at once imparted to intelligent strangers with the utmost liberality." Robert Kerr, *Memoirs of the Life, Writings and Correspondence of William Smellie* (1811)

12 TUESDAY

1790 Charles Elliot (b.1710), a major publisher of medical works, notably those of Alexander Monro I, William Cullen, James Gregory and James Lind, died. His most profitable medical publication was probably Benjamin Bell's *A System of Surgery*.

13 WEDNESDAY

1787 Members of the Grand Lodge of Scotland joined in a toast offered by the Grand Master to Caledonia and Robert Burns, the Caledonian Bard.

1831 The author of *The Man of Feeling*, Henry Mackenzie, died aged 86, in Edinburgh. *The Man of Feeling* was published anonymously in London in 1771 and sold out in under two months.

1778 The trial of Joseph Knight, a Negro of Africa, versus John Wedderburn of Ballindean, began in Edinburgh. Knight was the first black man in a Scottish civil court case to win his right to freedom.

1809 Commander in Chief at the Battle of Corunna, Glasgow-born Sir John Moore (b.1761), died on the battlefield. Sir John Hope, 4th Earl of Hopetoun, took charge for the final victory.

1746 On a wet and windy day in Falkirk the Jacobite forces were victorious over the Hanoverians led by General Henry Hawley. Hawley had replaced General Sir John Cope after the defeat at Prestonpans in 1745.

18 MONDAY
Martin L. King's Birthday
(USA)

1782 Sir John Pringle (b.1707), the Scots-born 'father of military medicine' and an originator of the concept of the International Red Cross, died in London after suffering what was probably a stroke at Watson's Club in The Strand.

19 TUESDAY

1736 The great engineer James Watt (d.1819) was born in Greenock. Inventor of the first efficient steam engine, Watt also devised a letter-copying press, used by his friends Joseph Black and William Cullen.

20 WEDNESDAY

1775 "I thought your book an imposture. I think it an imposture still," said Samuel Johnson to James 'Ossian' MacPherson. Despite such harsh words MacPherson lies close to Johnson in Westminster Abbey.

THURSDAY *21*

1793 At a quarter past ten, to the tuck of drums and before a cheering crowd in the Place de la Revolution, citizen Louis Capet, otherwise Louis XVI, was guillotined in Paris.

FRIDAY *22*

1788 Birthday of George Gordon Byron, Lord Byron (d.1824). He left Scotland aged ten but always considered himself as "born half a Scot and bred a whole one". Despite ridicule in the House of Lords for his Scottish accent, he maintained it all his life.

SATURDAY *23*

1753 Adam Smith read a paper on Hume's *Essays on Commerce* to the Literary Society of Glasgow.

SUNDAY *24*

1783 A few years after her sojourn in Edinburgh, The Duchess Ekaterina Dashkova was appointed president of the St Petersburg Academy of Arts and Sciences.

January 2010

25 MONDAY

1759 A 'waly boy' named Robert Burns (d.1796) was born at Alloway in Ayrshire. On the same date in 1817 The *Scotsman* newspaper was first published in Edinburgh.

26 TUESDAY
Australia Day (AUS)

1748 One of the ardent supporters of trial by jury, Allan Maconochie (d.1816), Lord Meadowbank, was born. Lord Brougham called him "the most diligent judge one can remember in the practice of Scottish law". On the same date in 1722 Alexander "Jupiter" Carlyle was born.

27 WEDNESDAY

1783 The *Glasgow Advertiser*, later known as the *Glasgow Herald* was first published by John Mennons to compete with the *Glasgow Journal* and *Glasgow Mercury*.

THURSDAY *28*

1829 From a High Street window, Sir Walter Scott and Charles Kirkpatrick Sharpe witnessed William Burke, of the infamous Burke and Hare partnership, being hanged on the gallows in Edinburgh.

FRIDAY *29*

1737 Thomas Paine (d.1809), son of a corset-maker, was born. His *Rights of Man* was widely read in Scotland and was also translated into Gaelic for its Highlander audience.

SATURDAY *30*

1805 One of the first conspiracy theorists, John Robison (b.1739), Professor of Natural Philosophy in Edinburgh, died at his home in the capital. He was also an accomplished musician and linguist.

SUNDAY *31*

1781 An advert appeared in the *Edinburgh Evening Courant* offering the lease of the Hall of the Royal Company of Archers for use as a tavern.

February 2010

1 MONDAY

1826 A large public meeting in Edinburgh chaired by the Earl of Rosebery was held to petition for the mitigation and ultimate abolition of slavery in the West Indies.

2 TUESDAY

1715 There was praise for the poet as Allan Ramsay (1686–1758) was made Laureate of the Easy Club in Edinburgh.

3 WEDNESDAY

1809 Composer Felix Mendelssohn (d.1847) was born. Inspired by a visit to Holyrood Abbey, he later wrote, "I believe I have found today in that old chapel the beginning of my Scottish Symphony."

THURSDAY 4

"It is to Sir James Wylie that Russia is indebted for the organisation of her medical schools," wrote Shaw Lefevre. A medical graduate of Aberdeen, Wylie went on to become physician to Tsars Paul and Alexander. He performed 200 operations in the field at the Battle of Borodino in 1812.

Lower L VI tooth extracted in Beckenham
Requested prescription for seretide
and pantoprazole.

FRIDAY 5

1723 John Witherspoon (d.1794) was born in Gifford near Edinburgh. The only clergyman to sign the *Declaration of Independence*, he was, in the words of John Adams, "as high a son of Liberty as any man in America".

1/ Write to library re: address
2/ check re: I instalment y sales

not Mark Thomson but ...... ?
Sadg said she could not go to the bank
today but wd pay for the two lessons on
Monday

SATURDAY 6
Waitangi Day (NZ)

1787 Robert Burns requested permission from the Bailies of the Canongate to raise a stone on Robert Fergusson's unmarked grave. The work was duly completed yet Burns took five years to settle the bill.

SUNDAY 7

"Il n'y a que les passions et les grandes passions, qui puissent élever l'âme aux grandes choses."
Denis Diderot, *Pensées Philosophiques* (1746)

February 2010

8 MONDAY

According to Lord Cockburn, "Classical learning, good conversation, excellent suppers, and ingenious though unsound metaphysics were the peculiarities of (Lord) Monboddo."

Dental appt.

Wednesday premier research or
(Kirin Elliot , 01926826784)
Called today at 8³⁰ pm with
telephone questionaire .

9 TUESDAY

"The progress of the arts and science is greatly accelerated by the history of antiquity and of nature." Reverend David Ure (1750–1798), 'father of Scottish palaeontology'

10 WEDNESDAY

1821 Writing from Edinburgh, Thomas Carlyle complained to John Aitken, "I have scarcely been one day right, since I came back to this accursed, stinking, reeking mass of stones and lime and dung."

THURSDAY 11

1790 The Society of Religious Friends, known as Quakers, petitioned Congress in the United States for the abolition of slavery.

[handwritten notes: Surgery nursery 3^{00} Kamna 4^{10} Vijay]

[handwritten notes: BBC QTime 18/3/81]

FRIDAY 12

1809 Two great men share a birthday on this date: Charles Darwin and Abraham Lincoln.

SATURDAY 13

1728 The 'father of scientific surgery', John Hunter (d.1793), younger brother of William, was born in East Kilbride. His first book, *Natural History of Human Teeth*, was published in 1771.

SUNDAY
St Valentine's Day 14

1779 A tragic end for the great Captain James Cook (b.1728), who was murdered by natives in Hawaii. Cartographer, explorer and son of a Scotsman, he joined HMS *Solway* as master in Leith in 1757.

February 2010

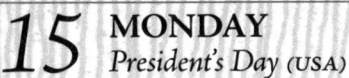

15 MONDAY
President's Day (USA)

1827 Sir Walter Scott wrote in his journal, "I make it a rule, seldom to read and never to answer foreign literary folk."

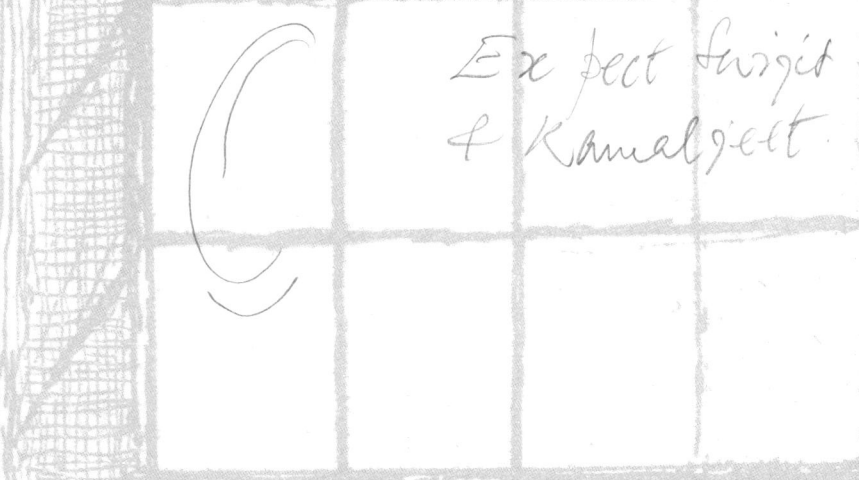

*Ex pect twrget
+ Kamaljeet*

16 TUESDAY

1785 Robert Buchanan (d.1873) was born in Callander. Professor of Logic and Rhetoric at Glasgow University, he earned the soubriquet 'Logic Bob'.

17 WEDNESDAY

1776 The first of six volumes of *The Decline and Fall of the Roman Empire* by Edward Gibbon was published. Nearly 1,000 copies were sold in the first six weeks. The last volume was published in May 1788.

1786 "A thousand things occur that would pass unnoticed by good easy people who are contented with trudging on the beaten path, but I am not contented until I can reason on every particular." Thomas Telford, engineer, in a letter to his friend Andrew Little

1717 First star of the British theatre, David Garrick, was born. He considered theatrical matters to be ill-managed in Scotland and protested to James Boswell, "Your directors are too great rakes, and too fine gentlemen, to serve themselves or please their audience."

1765 Writing from Nice, Tobias Smollett mentioned the necessary expense of employing an antiquarian "when a person wants to become a connoisseur in painting, statuary and architecture".

1826 John Kay (b.1742), barber, miniaturist and social commentator died at 227 High Street, Edinburgh and was buried in the northwest corner of Greyfriars Kirkyard.

February 2010

22 MONDAY

1808 Sir Walter Scott's *Marmion* was published in Edinburgh. It sold 2,000 copies in two months and remained a bestseller for the rest of the century.

23 TUESDAY

1827 At a Theatrical Fund Dinner in the Assembly Rooms in Edinburgh 300 male guests heard Sir Walter Scott admit authorship of *Waverley*.

24 WEDNESDAY

1776 Archibald Constable (d.1827), publisher, was born at Kellie in Fife. Scott remembered him thus: "How he swelled and rolled and reddened and outblarneyed all blarney."

THURSDAY *25*

"Hume is our Politics, Hume is our Trade, Hume is our Philosophy, Hume is our Religion."
James Hutchison Stirling, physician and philosopher from Glasgow

---

FRIDAY *26*

1792 The earliest minute records that on this date, at the behest of Andrew Duncan Senior, the Lord Provost of Edinburgh called a meeting of the Association for Instituting a Lunatic Asylum in Edinburgh.

SATURDAY *27*

"Truth springs from argument amongst friends." David Hume

SUNDAY *28*

1731 Birth of Carlo Giovanni Maria Denina (d.1813), Italian historian who believed that "the principal authors who have adorned the British literature ... have received their birth and education in Scotland."

March 2010

1 MONDAY

"The diplomatic character is of itself the narrowest sphere of society that man can act in. It forbids intercourse by the reciprocity of suspicion; and a diplomatic is a sort of unconnected atom, continually repelling and repelled." Thomas Paine, *The Rights of Man* (1795)

2 TUESDAY

1788 Robert Burns wrote to Clarinda (Mrs McElhose), "I shall be in Edinburgh next week. I long to see you." He gave his name as Sylvander.

3 WEDNESDAY

1777 James Boswell recalled his last visit to David Hume, describing the great philosopher as "lean, ghastly and quite of an earthy appearance".

THURSDAY 4

1756 Scotland's most famous portrait painter Sir Henry Raeburn (d.1823) was born in Edinburgh. During his lifetime he painted over 700 portraits, including four of Sir Walter Scott.

FRIDAY 5

1771 Robert Fergusson's *Elegy on the Death of Scots Music* was published in Ruddiman's *Weekly Magazine*.

SATURDAY 6

"On dit quelquefois: le sens commun est fort rare." Voltaire

SUNDAY 7

1792 William Robertson wrote to Andrew Dalziel of the demise of Robert Adam, "For genius, worth and for agreeable manners, I know none whom I should rank above the friend we have lost … "

March 2010

8 MONDAY

1773 Robert Fergusson's *The Rising of the Session* was published in Ruddiman's *Weekly Magazine*.

9 TUESDAY

1776 *The Wealth of Nations* by Adam Smith was published in two volumes by Strahan and Cadell. This edition had no preface or index, however it remains a key text of the Scottish Enlightenment.

10 WEDNESDAY

1748 John Playfair (d.1817), mathematician and Professor of Natural Philosophy at Edinburgh was born at Benvie, near Dundee. He wrote *Illustrations of the Huttonian Theory of the Earth* (1802).

1820 The explorer Sir Alexander Mackenzie, from the Isle of Lewis, died at the early age of 56. He completed the first overland crossing of North America in 1793. The Mackenzie River in Canada is named after him.

1755 The Select Society of Edinburgh declared that The Edinburgh Society for Encouraging Arts, Science, Manufactures and Agriculture in Scotland should be separated from the Select Society as an entity.

1812 Emotions ran high in the capital as Sarah Siddons gave her farewell performance at the Theatre Royal in Edinburgh. Her very last appearance was on the 9th of June 1819 as Lady Randolph in John Home's *Douglas*, for the benefit of Mr and Mrs Charles Kemble.

1778 The Incorporation of Surgeons became The Royal College of Surgeons of the city of Edinburgh by Royal Charter. Previously the Royal College of Physicians of Edinburgh had been founded in 1681.

15 **MONDAY**

1826 A sad day for Sir Walter Scott, then in financial difficulties, as he moved out of "poor No 39", his home in Castle Street, Edinburgh for over twenty years.

16 **TUESDAY**

Adam Smith described his friend David Hume "as approaching as nearly to the idea of a perfectly wise and virtuous man, as perhaps the nature of human frailty will permit".

17 **WEDNESDAY**
St. Patrick's Day (IRL)

1780 Thomas Chalmers (d.1847), social reformer and first Moderator of the Free Church of Scotland, was born in Anstruther. Port Chalmers in New Zealand is named after him.

THURSDAY *18*

1763 Dr Thomas Reid wrote to David Hume from the Philosophical Society of Aberdeen (f.1758), "If you write no more in morals, politics or metaphysics, I am afraid we shall be at a loss for subjects."

FRIDAY *19*

1721 Tobias Smollett (d.1771), physician and author who penned the famous phrase about Edinburgh, "a hot-bed of genius", was born in Renton, near Dumbarton. He also translated Cervantes' *Don Quixote*.

SATURDAY *20*

1727 Sir Isaac Newton (b.1643) died. His laws of motion and universal gravitation provided the foundation of classical mechanics. Scots Newtonians Archibald Pitcairne and David Gregory pre-deceased Newton.

SUNDAY *21*

1799 The first public notice of the Pneumatic Institute for inhalation gas therapy appeared in the *Bristol Gazette*. Staff included Edinburgh-trained Dr Thomas Beddoes and Dr 'Thesaurus' Roget.

March 2010

22 **MONDAY**

1832 Goethe died, aged 83 years. Scott, who usually resisted correspondence with 'foreign literary folk', made an exception for Goethe, whom he considered to be "different and a wonderful fellow."

23 **TUESDAY**

"The omnipotence of public opinion was not felt, nor thoroughly understood, till the *Edinburgh Review* came forth to enlighten, animate, and direct the mass of the community." Maurice Cross (1835)

24 **WEDNESDAY**

1776 John Harrison, the clockmaker, who constructed the first reliable marine chronometer which permitted the accurate computation of longitude, died in London on his 83rd birthday.

THURSDAY *25*

1784 Lord Gardenstone, Robert Grahame of Gartmore and others attended the first Convention of the Burgh Reform Group in Edinburgh. William Charles Little of Liberton presided over the meeting.

FRIDAY *26*

1797 James Hutton (b.1726), the father of modern geology, died. A few months later another Scottish geologist, Sir Charles Lyell, was born near Kirriemuir.

SATURDAY *27*

1760 Glasgow University was granted land known as 'The Butts' for "the better protection" of the new Macfarlane Observatory. Alexander Macfarlane donated his astronomical collection to the university.

SUNDAY *28*
British Summer
Time begins

1798 The 'Father of Scottish Palaeontology', the Rev. David Ure, died aged 48 years. His classic work, *The History of Rutherglen and East-Kilbride*, was published in 1793.

March 2010

29 MONDAY

1822 The librarian of King's College, Aberdeen, Ewan MacLachlan (b.1775) died. His great achievement was the translation of Homer's works into Gaelic.

30 TUESDAY

1825 Henry Brougham received the Freedom of the City of Edinburgh. Expressing gratitude to the city for his education he declared: "A school like the old High School of Edinburgh is invaluable, and for what is it so? It is because men of the highest and lowest rank in society send their children to be educated there."

31 WEDNESDAY

1732 The 'Father of the Symphony and String Quartet', Haydn (d.1809) was born in Austria. He arranged almost 400 Scottish songs for piano, violin and cello, half of which were commissioned by the Edinburgh publisher, George Thomson.

THURSDAY 1

1737 David Martin (d.1797) was born in Anstruther. He made the Grand Tour with his tutor Allan Ramsay and painted many of the great figures of the Enlightenment, including David Hume and Joseph Black.

FRIDAY 2
Good Friday (UK)

1821 James Gregory, Professor of the Practice of Medicine at Edinburgh, died aged 68 years. 'Worthy Gregory's Latin Face' was well known at William Creech's bookshop while Gregory's Mixture was the standard purgative to be found in any medicine cabinet.

SATURDAY 3

"Metaphysics in Muslin" was the description given of Maria Dundas, later Lady Callcott, a favourite of Edinburgh literary society, by Dr Thomas Brown, physician and metaphysician in Edinburgh.

SUNDAY 4
Easter Sunday

1765 The minute of a meeting at Glasgow University records the appointment of Robert Foulis to supply "a copperplate of the University Arms, an impression of which is to be pasted on every book".

5 MONDAY
Public Holiday (UK *not* SCO)

1739 Sir William Forbes of Pitsligo (d.1806), banker and philanthropist, was born in Edinburgh. He considered the choice of a business partner, in importance, to be "next to the choice of a wife".

6 TUESDAY

"Wisdom denotes the pursuing of the best ends by the best means." Frances Hutcheson, *An Enquiry into the Origins of our Ideas of Beauty and Virtue* (1725)

7 WEDNESDAY

1718 Hugh Blair (d.1800), Professor of Rhetoric and Belles Lettres, was born in Edinburgh. Samuel Johnson wrote of Blair's *Sermons*, "I love Blair's Sermons, though the dog is a Scotsman and a Presbyterian and everything he should not be."

THURSDAY *8*

"It was in society alone, by the mutual communication and reflection of the lights of reason and knowledge, that the intellectual as well as the moral powers of man are exalted and perfected," proposed Gilbert Blane to the Royal Medical Society in April 1775.

FRIDAY *9*

"The more enquiries, unbiased by theories, we make, and the greater number of facts that are undisguisedly related, the more able, surely, will mankind be to discover the phenomena by which the globe of the earth was thrown into its present state". Rev. David Ure (1793)

SATURDAY *10*

1784 The Irish-born politician and philosopher Edmund Burke was installed as Rector of Glasgow University, after spending some days with his friend Adam Smith in Edinburgh.

SUNDAY *11*

1816 Thomas Hay, President of the Royal College of Surgeons of Edinburgh in 1784 and 1794, died at his home in George Street, Edinburgh.

April 2010

12 MONDAY

1817 The celebrated French astronomer, Charles Messier (b.1730), described by Louis XV as the "ferret of comets", died in Paris and was buried in Père Lachaise cemetery. That same year John Smith & Son in Glasgow published *A Series of Discourses on the Christian Revelation viewed in connexion with the Modern Astronomy* by the Rev. Thomas Chalmers, first Moderator of the Free Church of Scotland.

13 TUESDAY

1728 James Gregory (1705–1755) was awarded his M.D. from King's College, Aberdeen. He followed his father as Professor of Medicine at King's College, Aberdeen, until his death, when his brother took the Chair for a further ten years.

14 WEDNESDAY

1721 George Turnbull, author of *Observations on Liberal Education*, was made Regent at Marischal College in Aberdeen. On the same date in 1759 Handel (b.1685) died in London, bequeathing a copy of his *Messiah* to the Foundling Hospital. Though he never visited Scotland, Handel and Allan Ramsay moved in similar circles and shared mutual friends.

1710 Described as a "medical faculty in himself", William Cullen (d.1790) was born in Hamilton, near Glasgow. On this same date in 1755 Samuel Johnson's *Dictionary of the English Language* was published in London, six years after the original deadline.

1728 William Cullen had just turned eighteen on the day before Joseph Black (d.1799), the chemist, was born in Bordeaux. On the same date in 1746 the Duke of Cumberland won the Battle of Culloden.

1767 The Town Council of Edinburgh announced that James Craig had been awarded the prize for a design for the New Town. Craig's final resting place, however, is the Old Town, in Greyfriars Kirkyard.

1765 James Boswell was favoured with a preview of Batoni's famous portrait of the Honourable William Gordon when he visited the artist's studio in Rome.

April 2010

19 MONDAY

1813 Benjamin Rush (b.1745) died in Philadelphia. Known as the 'father of American psychiatry', he took his M.D. at Edinburgh and was the only medic to sign the Declaration of Independence.

20 TUESDAY

1825 Sir Henry Jardine was knighted. When the crown jewels were unveiled at Edinburgh Castle in 1818, Sir Henry was first to hold aloft the Scottish Crown.

21 WEDNESDAY

1787 Perhaps as a present to himself on his 45th birthday, William Creech published the Edinburgh edition of Burns's *Poems, chiefly in the Scottish Dialect*. Also in this edition appeared 'To A Haggis'.

THURSDAY *22*

1774 The last issue of just thirteen numbers of *The Gentleman and Ladies Magazine* was published by James Tytler. The publication failed as it could not compete with the popular *Weekly Magazine*.

FRIDAY *23*

1762 A literary society gathering in Glasgow was first to hear Joseph Black read an account of his successful experiments on latent heat.

SATURDAY *24*

"Nous nous tournons vers l'Écosse pour trouver toutes nos idées sur la civilisation." Voltaire

SUNDAY *25*
Anzac Day (AUS & NZ)

1792 Captain Claude-Joseph Rouget de Lisle completed a patriotic tune first entitled *Chant de guerre de l'armée du Rhin*, now better known as *La Marseillaise*.

April 2010

26 MONDAY

1710 Thomas Reid (d.1796), the chief representative of the Scottish School of Common Sense, was born in Aberdeen. The following year, on the same date, David Hume (d.1776), philosopher and historian, was born in Edinburgh.

27 TUESDAY

In a letter of April 1821, advising the poet Shelley to be ever prepared for harsh reviews, Lord Byron wrote: "In this world of bustle and broil, and especially in the career of writing, a man should calculate upon his powers of resistance before he goes into the arena."

28 WEDNESDAY

1742 Henry Dundas, Viscount Melville, was born in Edinburgh. Also known as 'King Harry the Ninth', it was he who persuaded Pitt to issue a proclamation against seditious writings, which only led to an increase in sales of Paine's *Rights of Man*.

THURSDAY 29

1752 Adam Smith was transferred from the Chair of Logic at Glasgow University to the Chair of Moral Philosophy previously held by his esteemed teacher, Frances Hutcheson.

FRIDAY 30

1728 The world's first overdraft facility was created when William Hogg, a merchant of good standing, was allowed to borrow £1000 (about £60,000 in today's money) more than he had deposited at the Royal Bank of Scotland.

SATURDAY 1

1707 The Act of Union between Scotland and England came into force after long negotiations between English and Scottish commissioners were held in the Cockpit, a government building in Whitehall.

SUNDAY 2

1729 The 'philosopher on the throne', Catherine the Great (d.1796) was born. Many Scots engineers and medical men went to Russia during her reign. Three of her Scots doctors, Drs Matthew Halliday, James Mounsey and John Rogerson, hailed from Lochmaben in Dumfriesshire.

May 2010

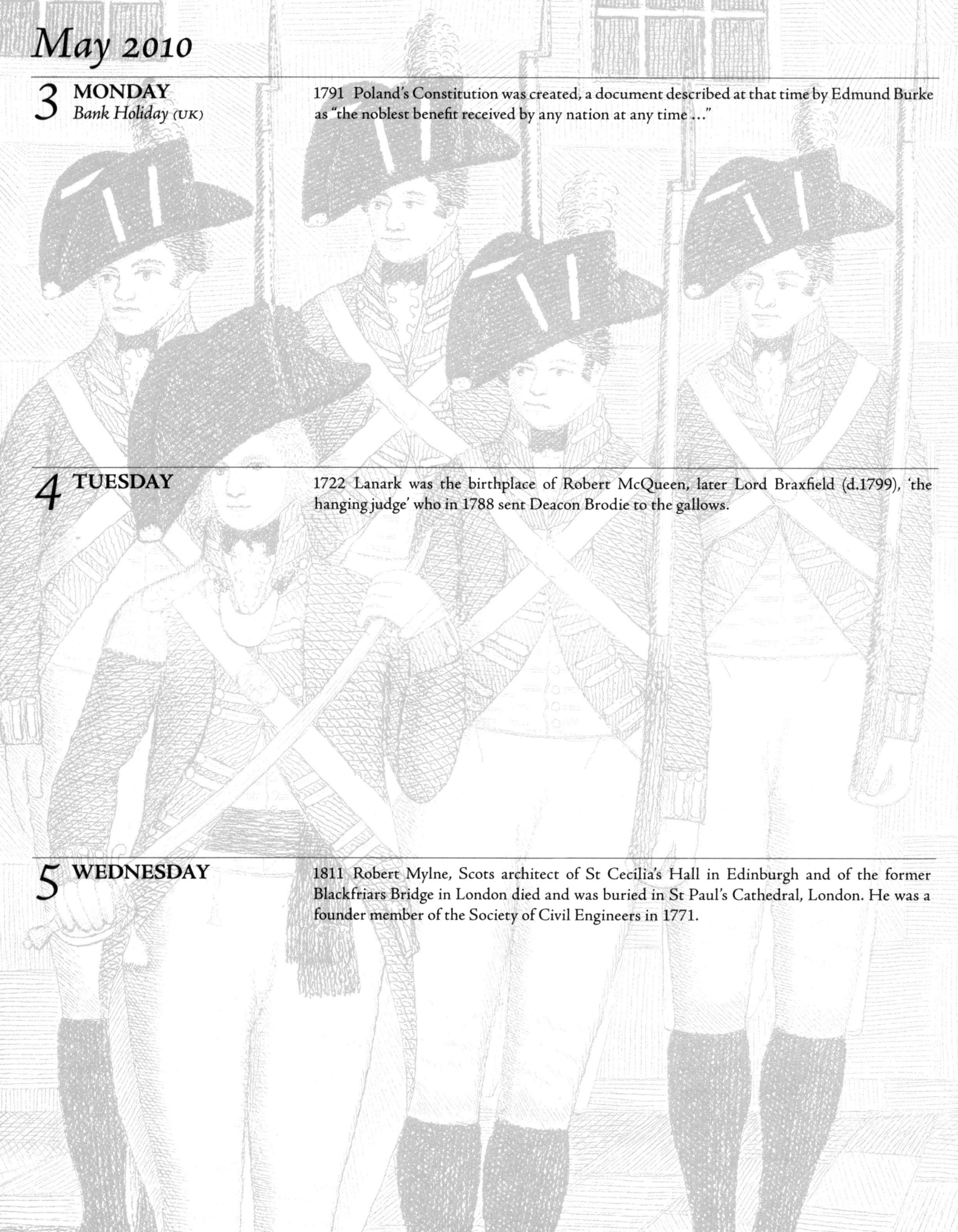

3 MONDAY
Bank Holiday (UK)

1791 Poland's Constitution was created, a document described at that time by Edmund Burke as "the noblest benefit received by any nation at any time …"

4 TUESDAY

1722 Lanark was the birthplace of Robert McQueen, later Lord Braxfield (d.1799), 'the hanging judge' who in 1788 sent Deacon Brodie to the gallows.

5 WEDNESDAY

1811 Robert Mylne, Scots architect of St Cecilia's Hall in Edinburgh and of the former Blackfriars Bridge in London died and was buried in St Paul's Cathedral, London. He was a founder member of the Society of Civil Engineers in 1771.

"It is not from the benevolence of the butcher, the brewer, or the baker, that we expect our dinner but from their regard to their own self-interest. We address ourselves, not to their humanity but to their self-love, and never talk to them of our own necessities but of their advantages." Adam Smith

1759 John Beugo, engraver of the Nasmyth portrait for the Edinburgh edition of Burns's *Poems, chiefly in the Scottish Dialect*, was born in Edinburgh.

1794 With no hope of mercy from the judge who declared, "the Republic needs neither scientists nor chemists; the trial cannot be restrained", Antoine Lavoisier (b.1743) was beheaded in Paris.

"It took only a moment to cause this head to fall and a hundred years will not suffice to produce its like again." Jean Louis Lagrange of his colleague and friend, Lavoisier

May 2010

10 MONDAY   1762 "America has sent us many good things ... but you are the first philosopher, and indeed the first great man of letters, for whom we are beholden to her." David Hume, in a letter to Benjamin Franklin

11 TUESDAY   1771 The eruption of Vesuvius was witnessed and recorded by Sir William Hamilton (1731–1803) in a series of letters to the Royal Society which were later published as the *Campi Phlegraei* in 1776. A rare copy is kept in Glasgow University Library.

12 WEDNESDAY   1725 The Black Watch was one of six companies commissioned under General Wade to 'police' or 'watch' the Highlands.

Recalling the teaching skills of William Cullen, a pupil wrote that Chemistry "was by him rendered a study so pleasing, so easy and so attractive, that it is now prosecuted by numbers as an agreeable recreation".

1796 Edward Jenner (b.1749) received an M.D. from St Andrews. He is remembered today as the pioneer of smallpox vaccination and the father of immunology.

1788 The physician, inventor and pioneer of public health, Neil Arnott (d.1874), was born in Arbroath. He graduated M.D. from Aberdeen and moved to London, where his popular inventions included the Arnott Stove.

1763 Johnson and Boswell first met in a London bookshop and on the same date, twenty-eight years later, Boswell's *Life of Samuel Johnson*, 'the greatest biography of all time', was published.

May 2010

17 MONDAY

1824 One of Scotland's great book collectors and "a martyr to the gout", David Steuart, died in Edinburgh aged 77. His Gutenberg Bible and a Breviary by Nicolaus Jenson are two of the rarest items preserved in the National Library of Scotland.

18 TUESDAY

1803 Britain abandons the Treaty of Amiens and declares war on France.

19 WEDNESDAY

1795 At the age of 55, The 9th Laird of Auchinleck, James Boswell, passed away in London but was buried near the family seat at Auchinleck in Ayrshire.

THURSDAY *20*

1747 It was to be an expedition with a difference as James Lind, Scottish physician and pioneer of naval medicine, "took twelve patients in the scurvy on board the Salisbury at sea" and started the world's first clinical trial.

FRIDAY *21*

1767 Adam Smith was elected a Fellow of the Royal Society of London.

SATURDAY *22*

1784 Crowds flocked to see Sarah Siddons give her first performance in Edinburgh as Belvidera in *Venice Preserved*. On the same date in 1791 Robert Adam began his last visit to Scotland.

SUNDAY *23*

1718 William Hunter (d.1783), anatomist and elder brother of John, was born in East Kilbride. His collections formed the basis of the Hunterian Museum, which opened in 1807 at Glasgow University.

May 2010

24 MONDAY
Victoria Day (CAN)

1824 At Tanfield in Edinburgh, Sir Walter Scott laid the foundation stone of works for The Edinburgh Oil-Gas Company. Scott chose oil-gas to light his new home at Abbotsford.

25 TUESDAY

1788 A 'best-laid' plan of Robert Burns was given in a letter to James Johnson in which he stated that he would marry Jean Armour and "give her a 'legal' title to the best blood in my body; and so farewell Rakery!"

26 WEDNESDAY

1799 Lord Monboddo (b.1714) died in Edinburgh. Johnson wrote of him, "Other people have strange notions but they conceal them; if they have tails, they hide them; but Monboddo is as jealous of his tail as a squirrel."

THURSDAY *27*

1781 The last magazine issue of *The Mirror* appeared. Together with *The Lounger*, these works, both published by Creech, "afforded a source of great literary amusement to the Edinburgh public, and the anticipation of the pleasure of next week's *Mirror* or *Lounger* was universally felt".

FRIDAY *28*

1819 A charter of George III gave the Infirmary of Dundee the royal designation of Dundee Royal Infirmary and Asylum.

SATURDAY *29*

1791 Alexander Stevenson (b.1726), who succeeded Joseph Black in the Chair of Medicine at Glasgow, died. Dr John Moore lauded Stevenson as a man "with a vast deal of physic contain'd in his wig!"

SUNDAY *30*

1778 François-Marie Arouet, better known as Voltaire (b.1694), died in Paris and was buried in the Pantheon. Jean-Jacques Rousseau was laid to rest close by only a few months later.

May/June 2010

31 MONDAY
Bank Holiday (UK)
Memorial Day (USA)

1727 The Royal Bank of Scotland, established by Royal Charter, was the first to issue British banknotes bearing the monarch's head. Granted by George I, the charter was, however, not sealed until the reign of George II.

1 TUESDAY

1799 One of the most successful alumni of the Foulis Academy of Fine Arts in Glasgow, James Tassie (b.1735), died in London and was buried in Southwark. A leading portrait modeller, he made around 500 medallions of his contemporaries, including Adam Smith and Robert Adam.

2 WEDNESDAY

1776 Robert Foulis (b.1707), the Glasgow printer and bookseller, died. Already a qualified barber, in 1741 he turned to publishing and together with his brother Andrew produced many fine editions. They received a loan from Glasgow University in 1753 to set up an Academy of Fine Arts but the project failed after just two years.

THURSDAY *3*

1726 The author of the seminal work on geology, *Theory of the Earth*, James Hutton (d.1797), was born in Edinburgh. From his enquiries into the formation of the Earth's crust he concluded, "we find no vestige of a beginning, no prospect of an end".

FRIDAY *4*

1738 George III (d.1820) was born at Norfolk House in London. 'The King's Birthday in Edinburgh', was a mock-celebration poem by Robert Fergusson published in The *Weekly Magazine* in 1772.

SATURDAY *5*

1723 One of Kirkcaldy's famous sons, Adam Smith (d.1790), the author of *The Wealth of Nations*, was born. Another famous son was Robert Adam, the architect, born in 1728.

SUNDAY *6*

1796 The Count d'Artois, brother of the executed Louis XVI, arrived at the port of Leith. It marked the beginning of a period of exile for the future Charles X.

June 2010

7 MONDAY

1757 Resignation from his charge at Athelstaneford was the choice of John Home in order to avoid proceedings emanating from his controversial play, *Douglas*.

8 TUESDAY

1772 Robert Stevenson (d.1850) was born in Glasgow. He was engineer-in-charge of the Bell Rock (1811), the oldest existing rock lighthouse in Britain, "a ruddy gem of changeful light".

9 WEDNESDAY

1796 Anderson's Institution was established in Glasgow, "to be managed by 81 Trustees from nine classes: tradesmen, agriculturalists, artists, manufacturers or merchants, mediciners, lawyers, divines, natural philosophers, and kinsmen".

1723 Gaelic speaker, philosopher and historian, Adam Ferguson (d.1816) was born in Perthshire. His *Essay on the History of Civil Society* was published in 1767.

THURSDAY 10

1793 William Robertson (b.1721), minister, historian and Principal of Edinburgh University for over thirty years, died in Edinburgh. Edward Gibbon confessed, "The Praise which has ever been the most flattering to my ear is to find my own name associated with the names of Robertson and Hume."

FRIDAY 11

1806 Congratulatory addresses were issued by Edinburgh's Town Council on news of the acquittal of Henry Dundas, Viscount Melville, after Impeachment "for High Crimes and Misdemeanours".

SATURDAY 12

1831 A true heir of the Scottish Enlightenment, James Clerk Maxwell (d.1879) was born in India Street, Edinburgh. A statue of the famous physicist was erected in his home city in 2008.

SUNDAY 13

June 2010

14 MONDAY

1822 Charles Babbage first proposed his 'difference engine' in a paper to the Royal Astronomical Society. One of his earliest published works was 'An Examination of Some Questions Connected with Games of Chance' in *Transactions of the Royal Society of Edinburgh*, 9:153–177, published in 1821.

15 TUESDAY

1768 Former mathematics tutor to the Duke of Cumberland, James Short (b.1710), Scots telescope maker, died in London. He became a Fellow of the Royal Society at the young age of twenty-six.

16 WEDNESDAY

1761 Thomas Sheridan, father of R.B. Sheridan, referred to Edinburgh as "a second Athens" and delivered two courses of lectures, one on elocution, the other on the English tongue in the capital. Over 300 men of eminent "rank and abilities" in Edinburgh attended the classes, including a young James Boswell.

THURSDAY *17*

"Is it not strange that (at) a time when we have lost our Princes, our Parliaments, our independent government ... is it not strange, I say, that in the circumstances, we shou'd really be the people most distinguish'd for Literature in Europe?" David Hume

FRIDAY *18*

1815 A statue at Edinburgh Castle recalls a daring sergeant in the Royal North British Dragoons, Charles Ewart, who rode out this day to capture the standard of the French 45th Regiment at Waterloo.

SATURDAY *19*

The Political Economy Club of Glasgow founded by Andrew Cochrane "to inquire into the nature and principles of trade in all its branches" counted Adam Smith a member for his thirteen years in Glasgow.

SUNDAY *20*

1827 Charles de Rémusat and Louis de Guizard visited Sir Walter Scott at Abbotsford for breakfast. Scott lamented, "they stayed till twelve o'clock, which is scarce fair, and plagued me with compliments".

June 2010

21 MONDAY

1777 The first of 101 numbers of the second edition of the *Encyclopedia Britannica* was published in Edinburgh. The last number appeared on 18th September 1784. James 'Balloon' Tytler wrote much of this second edition with no acknowledgement and little recompense for the marathon task.

22 TUESDAY

1735 John Millar (d.1801), jurist and Regius Professor of Civil Law at Glasgow University, was born. His *Observations concerning the Distinction of Ranks in Society* was published in 1778.

23 WEDNESDAY

1784 A meeting of the Royal Society of Edinburgh took place in the University Library. Attendees included William Cullen, William Robertson, Alexander Monro I, John Robison, Hugh Blair, Adam Ferguson and Adam Smith. The Duke of Buccleuch was elected first President and John Robison general secretary.

1795 William Smellie (b.1740), the 'learned printer', died and was buried next to William and John Adam in Greyfriars Kirkyard.

"L'homme est né libre, et partout il est dans les fers." Jean-Jacques Rousseau

"Amid the feeble and effete periodicals of the day, it burst like a bombshell", was the description given by Chambers Encyclopedia on the launch of the *Edinburgh Review*.

1687 George Drummond (d.1766) was born at Newton Castle near Blairgowrie. Six times Lord Provost of the city, he was a visionary figure in Edinburgh during the Scottish Enlightenment.

June 2010

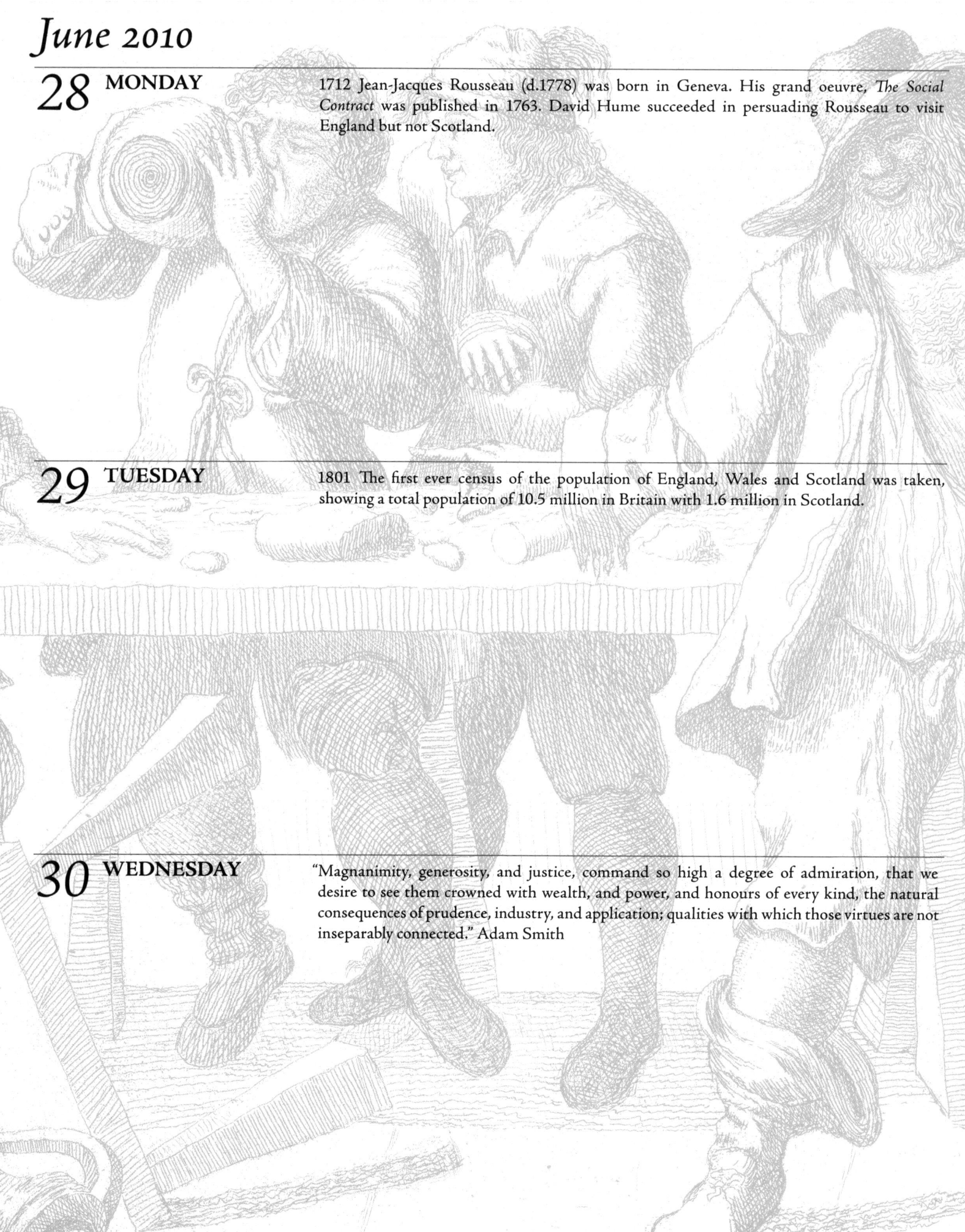

28 MONDAY

1712 Jean-Jacques Rousseau (d.1778) was born in Geneva. His grand oeuvre, *The Social Contract* was published in 1763. David Hume succeeded in persuading Rousseau to visit England but not Scotland.

29 TUESDAY

1801 The first ever census of the population of England, Wales and Scotland was taken, showing a total population of 10.5 million in Britain with 1.6 million in Scotland.

30 WEDNESDAY

"Magnanimity, generosity, and justice, command so high a degree of admiration, that we desire to see them crowned with wealth, and power, and honours of every kind, the natural consequences of prudence, industry, and application; qualities with which those virtues are not inseparably connected." Adam Smith

THURSDAY 1
Canada Day (CAN)

1791 James 'Balloon' Tytler launched his last Scottish publication, *The Historical Register*. Like many of his other projects, it failed. Success eluded Tytler all his life.

FRIDAY 2

1771 The Physico-Chirurgical Society, later The Physical Society, was founded in Edinburgh and merged with The Chirurgico-Medical Society in 1782.

SATURDAY 3

1728 Robert Adam (d.1792), the architect, was born in Kirkcaldy in Fife. In 1762 Piranesi dedicated his *Il Campo Marzio dell'antica Roma* thus: "al chiarissimo signore il sig. Roberto Adam".

SUNDAY 4
Independence Day

1776 *The Declaration of Independence* was approved by the Continental Congress. Signatories and later presidents, John Adams and Thomas Jefferson, both died on Independence Day in 1826.

July 2010

5 MONDAY
Holiday (USA)

1746 The new British Linen Bank in Edinburgh received its Royal Charter from George II.

6 TUESDAY

1747 The founder of the US Navy, John Paul Jones (d.1792), was born at Kirkbean in southwest Scotland. He died in Paris but was finally interred with full honours at Annapolis in the USA.

7 WEDNESDAY

1768 Edinburgh's popular weekly, *The Weekly Magazine or Edinburgh Amusement* was first published by Walter Ruddiman. It ran until June 1784.

THURSDAY 8

1823 Sir Henry Raeburn (b.1756) died and was buried in the dormitory graveyard of St. John's Episcopal Church in Edinburgh despite a family monument being in place at nearby St Cuthbert's Church.

FRIDAY 9

1785 Edinburgh-born William Strahan (b.1715), the most influential printer and publisher of his time, died in London. He was publisher and friend to Johnson, Smollett, Hume and Franklin.

SATURDAY 10

1786 Edinburgh Chamber of Commerce received its Royal Charter from George III. William Creech, bookseller and author, was its first secretary.

SUNDAY 11

1808 The end of a legal era came to Edinburgh with the Last Sitting of the Old Court of Session. Henceforth the Court would be split into the First and Second Divisions.

July 2010

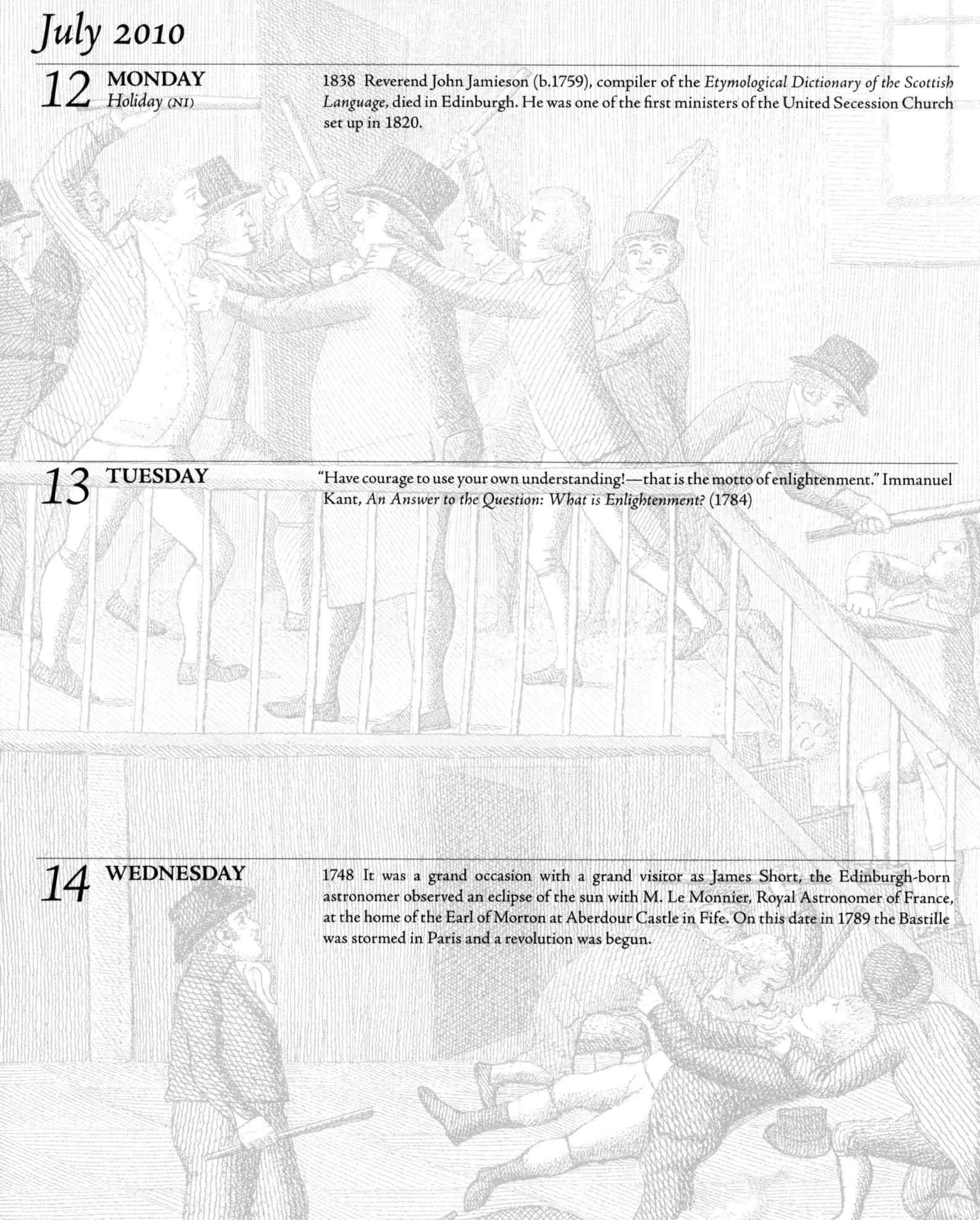

12 MONDAY
Holiday (NI)

1838 Reverend John Jamieson (b.1759), compiler of the *Etymological Dictionary of the Scottish Language*, died in Edinburgh. He was one of the first ministers of the United Secession Church set up in 1820.

13 TUESDAY

"Have courage to use your own understanding!—that is the motto of enlightenment." Immanuel Kant, *An Answer to the Question: What is Enlightenment?* (1784)

14 WEDNESDAY

1748 It was a grand occasion with a grand visitor as James Short, the Edinburgh-born astronomer observed an eclipse of the sun with M. Le Monnier, Royal Astronomer of France, at the home of the Earl of Morton at Aberdour Castle in Fife. On this date in 1789 the Bastille was stormed in Paris and a revolution was begun.

1805 Modern policing in Edinburgh took shape with the passing of the New Police Act.

1836 An Edinburgh merchant described John Kay's *Philosophers* thus: "Dr Black and Dr Hutton in close conversation at a table, with faces full of science."

1790 Adam Smith (b.1723) died at his home at Panmure House in Edinburgh and was buried a few yards away in the Canongate churchyard.

1794 James Lind, naval physician from Edinburgh, died at Gosport, Hampshire aged 78. Lind, a pioneer in the treatment of scurvy, completed the world's first clinical trial on HMS *Salisbury* in 1747.

July 2010

19 MONDAY

1809 Principal William Taylor of Glasgow University agreed to give up the cellar under Professor Mylne's dining room which he used as a brewhouse, but only on condition that it was returned to him once Professor Mylne had departed the building.

20 TUESDAY

1736 The jury at the trial of John Porteous in Edinburgh found him guilty "all in one voice" and he was condemned to death. He was later lynched by an angry mob and buried in Greyfriars Kirkyard.

21 WEDNESDAY

1796 Robert Burns died in Dumfries aged just 37, while his last child, Maxwell, was born on the day of his funeral a few days later on 25th July.

THURSDAY *22*

1793 Alexander Mackenzie from Lewis completed the first overland crossing of North America to reach the Pacific Ocean.

FRIDAY *23*

1745 The good ship *Du Teillay* brought Bonnie Prince Charlie to Eriskay on the west of Scotland.

SATURDAY *24*

"The Scots carry their pretensions to antiquity as high as any of their neighbours." Rev. William Robertson, *The History of Scotland* (1758)

SUNDAY *25*

1769 Boswell noted in his journal that he had taken part in a debate in Edinburgh where he had spoken against repealing the Marriage Act.

26 **MONDAY**

1792 First meeting in Scotland of the Society of the Friends of the People set up by Thomas Muir and William Skirving. Both were convicted of sedition in 1793.

27 **TUESDAY**

1777 Thomas Campbell (d.1844), poet, was born in Glasgow. Thomas Carlyle remarked, "There is a smirk on his face which would befit a shop man or an auctioneer." Campbell was Rector of Glasgow University and penned *Ye Mariners of England*.

28 **WEDNESDAY**

1825 The foundation stone of the new Royal High School in Edinburgh was laid. It was designed in a neoclassical Greek Doric style by Thomas Hamilton. He modelled the portico and Great Hall on the Hephaisteion of Athens. James VI gave the school the title "Schola Regia Edinensis" in 1590.

THURSDAY 29

1824 Lachlan Macquarie (b.1762), the 'father of Australia', was buried in Salen on his native Mull. This is supposed to be the first monument to have the word 'Australia' inscribed on it.

FRIDAY 30

"Here I stand at what is called the Cross of Edinburgh, and can in a few minutes take fifty men of genius by the hand." Amyot, the King's Chemist enthusing to William Smellie, the Edinburgh printer

SATURDAY 31

1786 *Poems, chiefly in the Scottish Dialect* by Robert Burns was published in Kilmarnock by John Wilson. There were 600 copies at a cost of three shillings each.

SUNDAY 1

1785 Lord Haddo, Grand Master Mason, laid the foundation stone for the new South Bridge in Edinburgh. Robert Kay, cousin of John Kay, was the architect.

August 2010

2 MONDAY
Bank Holiday (SCO)

1775 "I think your solution is just, but why think? Why not try the experiment?" wrote John Hunter, surgeon, in a letter to Edward Jenner about an experiment on a hedgehog.

3 TUESDAY

1796 The Town Council of Edinburgh agreed to award a grant of fifteen guineas to the Edinburgh Burgess Golfing Society. The first recorded reference to the club's existence since 1735 appeared in a nineteenth-century edition of the *Edinburgh Almanac*.

4 WEDNESDAY

1762 At the first election of the Select Society for Promoting the Reading and Speaking of the English Language in Scotland the Ordinary Directors included Hugh Blair, Dr William Robertson, Dr John Hope, John Adam and Adam Fergusson.

THURSDAY 5

Dougal Graham (1724–1779), a Glasgow-based writer of chapbooks, advertised his fourpenny *Impartial History of the Rise, Progress, and Extinction of the Late Rebellion in Britain in the Years 1745 and 1746* claiming, "The like has not been done in Scotland since the days of Sir David Lindsay."

FRIDAY 6

1729 A new Infirmary or Hospital for the Sick Poor was opened at the top of Robertson's Close in Edinburgh. It became the Royal Infirmary in 1736. Glasgow Royal Infirmary dates back to 1794.

SATURDAY 7

1776 In his will, David Hume left his friend John Home ten dozen "old claret, at his choice, and one single bottle of that other liquor, called port". Sadly, Home died on the 25th of the same month.

SUNDAY 8

1746 Frances Hutcheson, Professor of Moral Philosophy at Glasgow, died on his 52nd birthday. Known as the 'Dean of the Scottish Enlightenment', his most famous pupil was Adam Smith.

August 2010

9 MONDAY
1757 Thomas Telford, described by the poet Southey as the "Colossus of Roads", was born in Westerkirk, Dumfriesshire. He was engineer for 920 miles of new roads and 32 new churches in Scotland.

10 TUESDAY
1784 The great Scottish painter Allan Ramsay (b.1713) died at Dover. His friends included Diderot, Rousseau, Clerisseau and Voltaire. He refused a knighthood.

11 WEDNESDAY
1832 A Parade was held in Edinburgh to celebrate the passing of the Great Reform Act.

THURSDAY *12*

1772 Sir Joseph Banks visited Staffa and gave the first detailed account of the island and its famous landmark, Fingal's Cave. Mendelssohn's *Overture (Fingal's Cave), Op.26* was composed in 1830.

FRIDAY *13*

1765 With 33 casks of the blubber and the 'cring' of one whale as cargo, *The Royal Bounty* berthed in Leith. The surgeon on board was James 'Balloon' Tytler.

SATURDAY *14*

1773 Dr Samuel Johnson arrived in Edinburgh and stayed at Boyd's Inn in the Canongate.

SUNDAY *15*

1771 As a young Corsican named Napoleon Bonaparte celebrated his second birthday, Walter Scott (d.1832) was born in the Old Town of Edinburgh to Walter Scott W.S. and Anne Rutherford.

August 2010

16 MONDAY

1773 A contemporary reporter wrote of Johnson's visit to the Laigh Hall in Edinburgh, "I was pleased to behold Dr Samuel Johnson rolling about in this old Magazine of Antiquities."

17 TUESDAY

1822 A guest list of 2,000 noblemen and gentlemen assembled at Holyrood Palace to meet George IV clad in Highland dress. Some 500 ladies of rank had to wait a further three days to meet the King.

18 WEDNESDAY

1773 Boswell and Johnson set out from Edinburgh on their historic three-month tour of the Highlands and Inner Hebrides.

1819 James Watt (b.1736), the man with his name on every light bulb, died in Birmingham. Watt learnt German and Italian in order to read contemporary accounts of steam power.

"All the ends of speaking are reducible to four; every speech being intended to enlighten the understanding, to please the imagination, to move the passions, or to influence the will". George Campbell, *The Philosophy of Rhetoric* (1776)

1754 The Scot who 'lit the world', William Murdoch (d.1839), was born. His Rumford medal was for "both the first idea of applying, and the first actual application of gas to economical purposes".

1806 The Edinburgh East India Club gave 'an elegant entertainment' at Oman's tavern to Warren Hastings Esq., late Governor General of India, during his visit to the capital.

August 2010

23 MONDAY

1807 A pamphlet was published by James Miller M.D. and William Vuzie outlining the practicalities of tunnelling under the Firth of Forth.

24 TUESDAY

1822 The city of Edinburgh hosted a banquet for George IV in Parliament Hall and the newly completed Advocates Library was placed at the king's disposal as his retiring room.

25 WEDNESDAY

1744 Johann Herder (d.1803), the German philosopher and poet who publicised 'Ossian' in Germany, was born in Prussia. On the same date in 1776 Scotland's great philosopher, David Hume, died in Edinburgh. His mausoleum in Edinburgh's Old Calton Burial Ground was designed by Robert Adam.

THURSDAY *26*

1789 *The Declaration of the Rights of Man and the Citizen* was approved by the National Assembly of France in Paris.

FRIDAY *27*

1784 James Tytler, the first Scots aeronaut, ascended in his Great Fire Balloon from Comely Gardens, near Holyrood Palace. The balloon had been on public display inside the dome of the incomplete Register House.

SATURDAY *28*

1811 John Leyden (b.1775) of Denholm, polymath and close friend of Sir Walter Scott, died in Java. Lord Cockburn commented that, "there was no walk of life in which Leyden could not have shone".

SUNDAY *29*

1822 Sir Henry Raeburn received his knighthood from George IV at Hopetoun House. His Edinburgh tour over, the king visited Hopetoun en route to his ship at Port Edgar.

August/September 2010

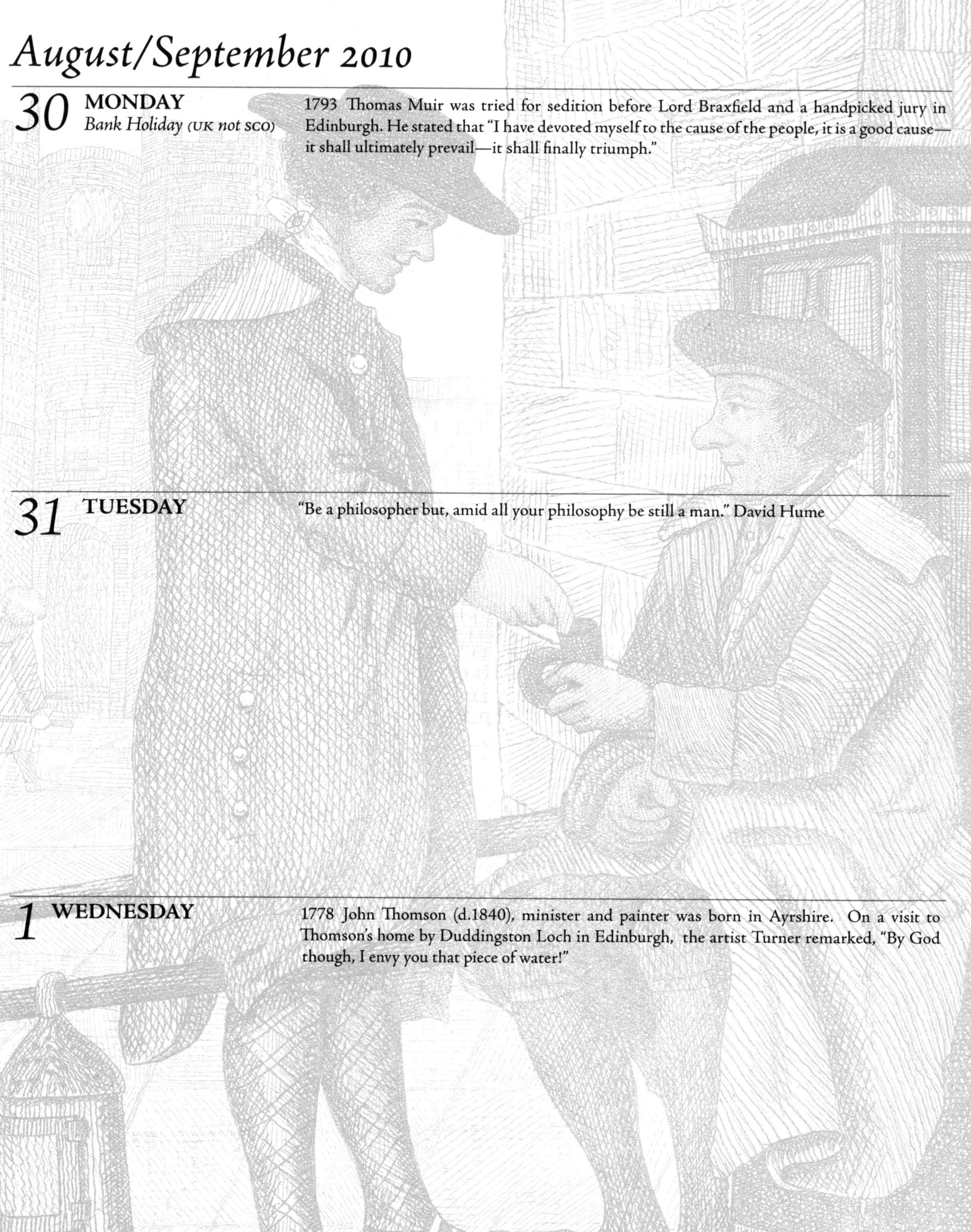

30 **MONDAY**
Bank Holiday (UK not SCO)

1793 Thomas Muir was tried for sedition before Lord Braxfield and a handpicked jury in Edinburgh. He stated that "I have devoted myself to the cause of the people, it is a good cause—it shall ultimately prevail—it shall finally triumph."

31 **TUESDAY**

"Be a philosopher but, amid all your philosophy be still a man." David Hume

1 **WEDNESDAY**

1778 John Thomson (d.1840), minister and painter was born in Ayrshire. On a visit to Thomson's home by Duddingston Loch in Edinburgh, the artist Turner remarked, "By God though, I envy you that piece of water!"

THURSDAY 2

1722 John Home (d.1808), minister and author of the controversial play *Douglas*, was born in Leith. The play evoked the famous comment, "Weel, lads, what think ye o' Wully Shakespeare noo?"

FRIDAY 3

1752 The Gregorian calendar was introduced to the dismay of many, who demanded, "Give us back our eleven days."

SATURDAY 4

Of the Meadows parkland in Edinburgh, Lord Cockburn wrote, "Under these trees walked, and talked, and meditated, all our literary and scientific, and many of our legal worthies."

SUNDAY 5

1750 Robert Fergusson (d.1774), poet, was born in Edinburgh. On the same date nine years later, Benjamin Franklin was given the Freedom of the City of Edinburgh and the Freedom of St Andrews.

September 2010

6 **MONDAY**
Labor Day (USA & CAN)

1715 The Earl of Mar unfurled the Standard of the Old Pretender at Braemar.

7 **TUESDAY**

1782 The novelist and great friend of Sir Walter Scott, Susan Ferrier (d.1854), was born in Edinburgh.

8 **WEDNESDAY**

1721 William Robertson, a key figure of the Scottish Enlightenment, was born at Borthwick near Edinburgh. Principal of Edinburgh University from 1762 until his death in 1793, he is buried in Greyfriars Kirkyard.

THURSDAY 9

1758 Alexander Nasymth (d.1840), painter, was born in the Grassmarket in Edinburgh. His portrait of Robert Burns remains the best-known image of the poet.

FRIDAY 10

1771 The Scots surgeon and explorer Mungo Park (d.1806), who discovered the source of the Blue Nile, was born at Foulshiels near Selkirk.

SATURDAY 11

"There was never a good war or bad peace." Benjamin Franklin

SUNDAY 12

1792 William Tytler (b.1711), the Scottish historian and antiquarian, died. He is best known for his *Historical and Critical Enquiry* concerning Mary, Queen of Scots, published in 1760.

September 2010

13 MONDAY

1753 The man who "changed the face of the metropolis", George Drummond, as Grand Master Mason, laid the foundation stone of the Royal Exchange in Edinburgh.

14 TUESDAY

1753 *A retrospective of the Public Buildings, and other external improvements, of the City of Edinburgh from 14th September 1753 to 9th July 1816, inclusive; being the result of 63 years of personal observation* was compiled by Thomas Sommers.

15 WEDNESDAY

1764 James Rae, a pioneer in the teaching of dentistry, was elected Deacon of the Incorporation of Surgeons. His elder son, William, was appointed Dentist to the King in 1785.

THURSDAY 16

1817 Thomas Sommers died. The friend and biographer of Robert Fergusson, his *Life of Robert Fergusson, the Scottish Poet* was published in 1803.

FRIDAY 17

1771 "Some folks are wise and some otherwise," wrote Tobias Smollett, who died on this day aged 50.

SATURDAY 18

1775 Andrew Foulis (b.1712), the younger brother of Robert, died. The brothers printed over 500 publications in Glasgow and enjoyed an international reputation for quality editions of the classics.

SUNDAY 19

1815 The foundation stone of the Regent Bridge in Edinburgh was laid by Sir John Marjoribanks, Lord Provost. The 60 foot-wide bridge was opened in 1819.

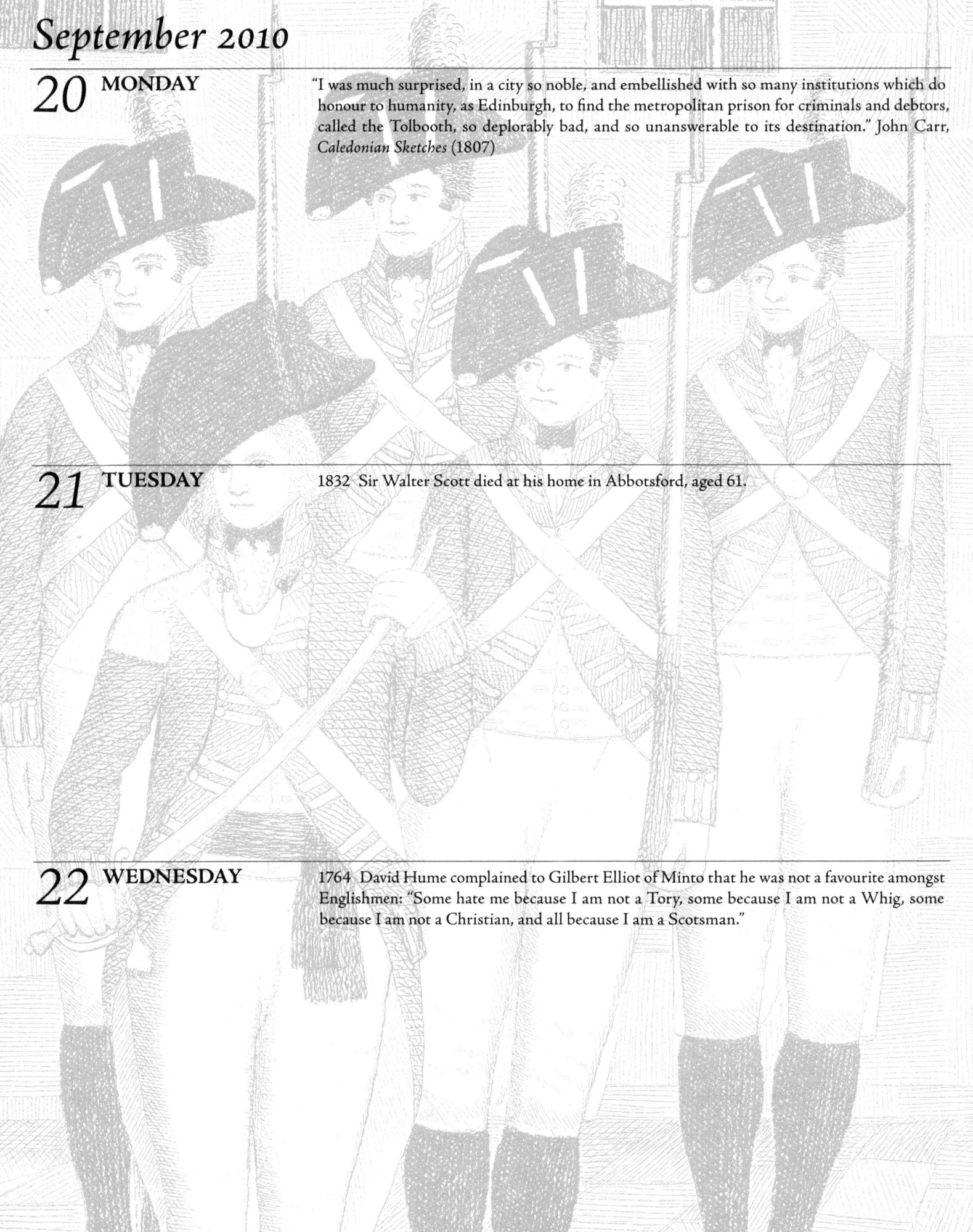

September 2010

20 MONDAY

"I was much surprised, in a city so noble, and embellished with so many institutions which do honour to humanity, as Edinburgh, to find the metropolitan prison for criminals and debtors, called the Tolbooth, so deplorably bad, and so unanswerable to its destination." John Carr, *Caledonian Sketches* (1807)

21 TUESDAY

1832 Sir Walter Scott died at his home in Abbotsford, aged 61.

22 WEDNESDAY

1764 David Hume complained to Gilbert Elliot of Minto that he was not a favourite amongst Englishmen: "Some hate me because I am not a Tory, some because I am not a Whig, some because I am not a Christian, and all because I am a Scotsman."

THURSDAY *23*

1786 Sir John Sinclair arrived in Kiev while on an extensive 8,000-mile tour around Europe. He called Catherine the Great a "hero in petticoats".

FRIDAY *24*

"Enlightenment is man's emergence from his self-incurred immaturity." Immanuel Kant, philosopher and grandson of a Scottish saddle-maker

SATURDAY *25*

1717 The start of a long career in public service to the capital, George Drummond was elected one of three merchant councillors of the Town Council of Edinburgh.

SUNDAY *26*

1726 John Anderson (d.1796), known to his students as 'Jolly Jack Phosphorous', was born near Glasgow. His executors founded Anderson's Institution, later part of the University of Strathclyde.

September 2010

27 MONDAY — 1742 Hugh Boulter (b.1672), Primate of Ireland and admirer of Francis Hutcheson, died, bequeathing £250 to Glasgow University to support a student from England or Ireland.

28 TUESDAY — Of the lectures in Moral Philosophy given by Dugald Stewart at Edinburgh, Lord Cockburn wrote, "His noble views, unfolded in glorious sentences, elevated me into a higher world ..."

29 WEDNESDAY — 1792 Dr John Moore, physician and author, along with Lord Lauderdale, witnessed the disturbances in Paris of 10th August and 29th September. Moore later published his record of these events as *A Journal during a residence in France* in 1793 and 1794.

THURSDAY *30*

1763 William Duff, 1st Earl of Fife, died aged 67. He commissioned one of Britain's finest Georgian mansions, Duff House, near Banff in Scotland. Designed by William Adam, it was completed in 1740.

FRIDAY *1*

1788 Deacon Brodie, whose double life inspired Robert Louis Stevenson, was hanged on the gallows which he had designed himself. Some say he survived and fled from Edinburgh to America.

SATURDAY *2*

1817 Alexander Monro II (b.1733) died in Edinburgh, and in the family tradition was succeeded in the Chair of Anatomy by his son, Alexander Monro III.

SUNDAY *3*

"Never literary attempt was more unfortunate than my Treatise of Human Nature. It fell *dead-born from the press*, without reaching such distinction, as even to excite a murmur among the zealots." David Hume

October 2010

4 MONDAY

1821 John Rennie (b.1761), the Scots engineer who designed Kelso Bridge, the old Waterloo Bridge and the New London Bridge (opened 1831), died in London and was buried in St Paul's Cathedral.

5 TUESDAY

1785 The flamboyant aeronaut Lunardi made his grand balloon ascent in Edinburgh from Heriot's Green. Many shops closed and an estimated crowd of 80,000 came to watch the spectacle.

6 WEDNESDAY

1742 Born in Kirkliston, Andrew Dalziel (d.1806), Professor of Greek at Edinburgh, was the first layman to hold the post of Principal Clerk to the General Assembly.

THURSDAY 7

1796 Thomas Reid, founder of the Scottish School of Common Sense, died in Glasgow, aged 86. Other 'common sense' philosophers included Dugald Stewart, James Beattie and George Campbell.

FRIDAY 8

1817 Henry Erskine (b.1746), Lord Advocate and the champion of rich and poor in the law courts, died at his home at Almondell, near Edinburgh.

SATURDAY 9

1777 The first issue of the *London Magazine* was published in October, with James Boswell contributing a column under the pseudonym The Hypochondriak.

SUNDAY 10

1802 The first issue of the *Edinburgh Review* drew support from Dr Thomas Chalmers: "May the young philosophers of Edinburgh succeed in their many and independent efforts at literary distinction."

October 2010

11 **MONDAY**
Columbus Day (USA)

1797 Forfar-born Admiral Duncan led the British Fleet to victory when they defeated the Dutch off Camperdown in Holland.

12 **TUESDAY**

"Edinburgh has long been celebrated for the variety and importance of its literary and scientific institutions, the reputation of its men of letters, and the intelligence of its population." Maurice Cross (1835)

13 **WEDNESDAY**

1713 Allan Ramsay (d.1784), the painter, was born in Edinburgh. Dr Johnson once remarked, "You will not find a man in whose conversation there is more instruction, more information and more elegance, than in Ramsay."

THURSDAY *14*

1788 Patrick Millar, entrepreneur, along with William Symington tested the first steamship at Dalswinton Loch on Millar's estate near Dumfries.

FRIDAY *15*

1739 James Anderson (d.1808), economist and agriculturist, was born at Hermiston, Midlothian. He had little formal education yet he published The *Bee* magazine, invented the Scotch Plough and received an honorary doctorate in Law from Aberdeen.

SATURDAY *16*

1774 Robert Fergusson died in Bedlam at the age of 24 and was buried in the Canongate Kirkyard. On the same date in 1793 John Hunter (b. 1728) was "brought home stone dead in a sedan chair".

SUNDAY *17*

1781 Lord Cornwallis wrote to George Washington asking for terms for a British surrender. After lengthy negotiation the Preliminary Articles of Peace were signed on the 30th November 1782.

October 2010

18 **MONDAY**   1766 Adam Smith's young charge, Hew Campbell Scott, the younger brother of the Duke of Buccleuch, was murdered in Paris.

19 **TUESDAY**   1819 A second Music Festival convened in Edinburgh, with six concerts being held in the Parliament Hall and in the theatre. A total of 8,526 people attended.

20 **WEDNESDAY**   "Few are so insensible, as not to be struck even at first view with what is truly sublime; and every person upon seeing a grand object is affected with something which as it were extends his very being, and expands it to a kind of immensity." John Baillie, *An Essay on the Sublime* (1747)

THURSDAY 21

1817 James Hogg's satirical Chaldee Manuscript appeared in *Blackwood's Magazine*. On the same date George Combe published his first essay on phrenology in the *Scots Magazine*.

FRIDAY 22

1746 A charter for the foundation of the College of New Jersey, later Princeton, was granted by George II under the seal of John Hamilton. John Witherspoon from Gifford, near Edinburgh, became 6th President of the College in 1766.

SATURDAY 23

1822 In readiness for the formal opening of the Caledonian Canal, designed by Thomas Telford, the 'Loch Ness Steam Yacht' departed the Muirton Locks at ten o'clock in the morning.

SUNDAY 24

1796 David Roberts (d.1864), landscape painter, was born in Duncan's Land in Edinburgh.

25 **MONDAY**   1714 Lord Monboddo (d.1799) was born at Monboddo House in Kincardineshire.

26 **TUESDAY**   1767 The foundation stone of Rose Court (now Thistle Court), the first building in the New Town of Edinburgh, was laid by James Craig, the architect.

27 **WEDNESDAY**   1761 Matthew Baillie (d.1823) was born in Shotts. His *Morbid Anatomy* was the first English text on the subject of pathology.

THURSDAY *28*

1794 Robert Liston (d.1847), surgeon, was born at Ecclesmachen near Linlithgow. His first operation using ether as an anaesthetic in 1846 was observed by a young Joseph Lister. Liston died a month after Simpson's experiment with chloroform.

FRIDAY *29*

1740 James Boswell (d.1795), Johnson's biographer, was born in Edinburgh at Blair's Land, near Parliament Square.

SATURDAY *30*

1787 Professor Dalziel reported that the University Mace had been stolen on "the night betwixt" the 29th and 30th October. Deacon Brodie, a patron of the Tounis College, was suspected of the theft.

SUNDAY
British Summer
Time ends
31

"Hatred and anger are the greatest poison to the happiness of a good mind." Adam Smith, *The Theory of Moral Sentiments* (1759)

November 2010

1 MONDAY

1768 The first known class ticket issued by the Royal Infirmary of Edinburgh was written out on a playing card, the ten of clubs.

2 TUESDAY

"Glasgow is, indeed, a very fine city; the four principal streets are the fairest for breadth, and the finest built that I have ever seen in one city together … In a word, 'tis the cleanest and beautifullest and best built city in Britain, London excepted." Daniel Defoe, writing about his visit to Glasgow in 1707

3 WEDNESDAY

1730 Irish-born Francis Hutcheson was appointed Professor of Moral Philosophy at the University of Glasgow, a post that he held until his death in 1747.

THURSDAY *4*

1774 "I went to Fortune's, found nobody in the house but Captain James Gordon of Ellon. He and I drank five bottles of claret and were most profound politicians." James Boswell's *Edinburgh Journals 1767–1786*

FRIDAY *5*

1819 Sir Henry Jardine, grandson of Provost George Drummond, was present at the opening of the grave of Robert the Bruce at Dunfermline Abbey.

SATURDAY *6*

1787 Burns wrote to James Hoy: "Those who think that composing a Scotch song is a trifling business—let them try."

SUNDAY *7*

George Birkbeck, Professor of Natural Philosophy at Anderson's Institution and founder of Birkbeck College, gave free classes to Glasgow workmen in 1800. The Mechanics Institute was created in 1823.

8 MONDAY

1736 Allan Ramsay opened the first regular public theatre in Scotland in Carruber's Close in the Old Town of Edinburgh.

9 TUESDAY

1776 Shortly after the death of Hume, Adam Smith wrote to the publisher William Strahan Esq., "His constant pleasantry was the genuine effusion of good nature and good humour, tempered with delicacy and modesty, and without even the slightest tincture of malignity, so frequently the disagreeable source of what is called wit in other men."

10 WEDNESDAY

1786 John Hope (b.1725), Professor of Botany and first Regius Keeper of the Royal Botanic Garden, died in Edinburgh and was buried in the northwest corner of Greyfriars Kirkyard.

1818 His Royal Highness The Archduke Maximilian of Austria was given the freedom of the City of Edinburgh.

1808 A month after the last sitting of the Old Court of Session, the new system of Two Divisions assembled for the first time.

1779 Thomas Chippendale (b.1718), cabinet-maker and interior designer, died in London. The most important collection of works from Chippendale's Director period are in Dumfries House in Scotland.

1770 James Bruce, Scots explorer, (1730–1794), reached Lake Tana, the source of the Blue Nile.

November 2010

15 MONDAY

1800 The Glasgow Police, formed as a result of the new Glasgow Police Act, assembled for the first time at the Session House of the Laigh Kirk in the Trongate.

16 TUESDAY

1789 Lord Napier laid the foundation stone of the New College on South Bridge, Edinburgh. Robert Adam, the architect, and William Robertson, principal of the University of Edinburgh, were present.

17 WEDNESDAY

1764 The Speculative Society, an elite debating society, was founded in Edinburgh. To this day it retains rooms in the Old College of the University of Edinburgh.

THURSDAY *18*

1761 John Robison (1739–1805) was sent by the Board of Longitude to monitor trials of a new chronometer built by John Harrison. He accompanied Harrison's son William on the trip to Jamaica.

FRIDAY *19*

"I am afraid of Kames' 'Law Tracts'. A man might as well think of making a fine sauce by a mixture of wormwood and aloes, as an agreeable composition by joining metaphysics and Scottish law." Hume, in a letter to Adam Smith

SATURDAY *20*

1786 Hugo Arnot (b.1749), author of the famous *History of Edinburgh*, died in Edinburgh and was buried in a grave of his own design at South Leith Kirkyard.

SUNDAY *21*

Lord Cockburn wrote of Francis Jeffrey's home at Craigcrook, "No unofficial house in Scotland has had a greater influence on literary or political opinion."

November 2010

22 **MONDAY**   1753 Dugald Stewart (d.1828), philosopher and 'teacher of genius', was born in Edinburgh. His monument on Calton Hill is a major landmark in Edinburgh.

23 **TUESDAY**   1785 After being on display in the choir of St Mungo's Cathedral, Lunardi's balloon was made ready and rose from St Andrew Square in Glasgow in full view of an estimated 100,000 spectators. It later landed in Hawick at the feet of some trembling shepherds.

24 **WEDNESDAY**   "Reason owes him incalculable obligations." Adam Smith of Voltaire

"Abair ach beagan is abair gu math e." (Say but little and say it well.) Gaelic Proverb

THURSDAY 25
Thanksgiving Day (USA)

1780 Sir James Denham Steuart (b.1713), author of *An Inquiry into the Principles of Political Economy*, died at the family home at Coltness in Lanarkshire.

FRIDAY 26

1778 John Murray (d.1843), eminent publisher, was born. The John Murray Archive in the National Library of Scotland is considered one of the world's greatest publishing archives.

SATURDAY 27

1786 The 'ploughman poet' Robert Burns arrived on the first of several visits to Edinburgh. He lodged with a friend, John Richmond in Baxter's Close in the Lawnmarket.

SUNDAY 28

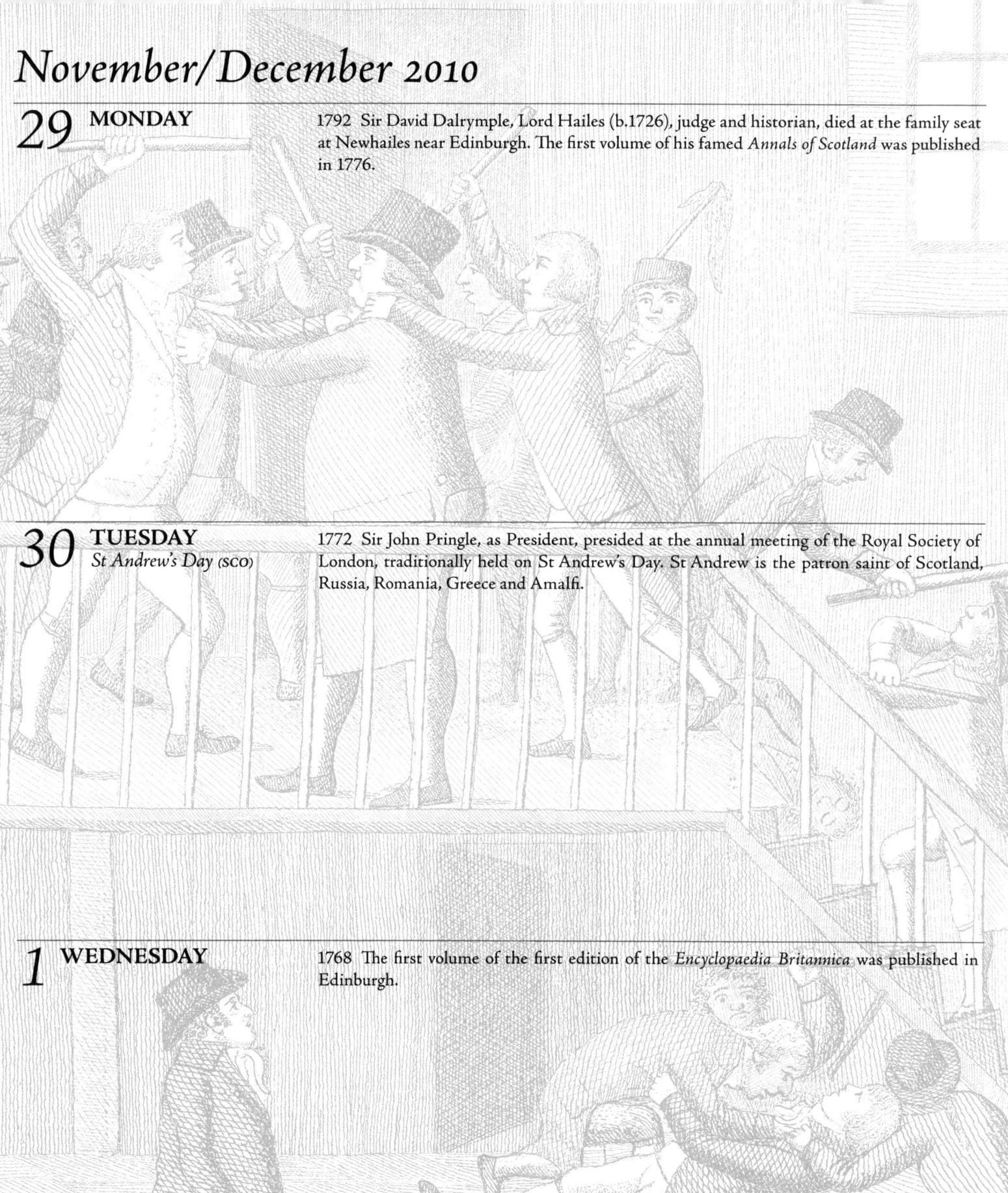

29 MONDAY

1792 Sir David Dalrymple, Lord Hailes (b.1726), judge and historian, died at the family seat at Newhailes near Edinburgh. The first volume of his famed *Annals of Scotland* was published in 1776.

30 TUESDAY
St Andrew's Day (SCO)

1772 Sir John Pringle, as President, presided at the annual meeting of the Royal Society of London, traditionally held on St Andrew's Day. St Andrew is the patron saint of Scotland, Russia, Romania, Greece and Amalfi.

1 WEDNESDAY

1768 The first volume of the first edition of the *Encyclopaedia Britannica* was published in Edinburgh.

THURSDAY 2

1786 Christmas came early for William Smellie when he was offered £1,000 in advance of publication by Charles Elliot for *The Philosophy of Natural History*. The first volume appeared in print in 1790 and the second in 1799.

FRIDAY 3

"Lord Hailes very readily agreed to my sending you a specimen of his *Annals of Scotland*. I give you a double treat. For I enclose you a specimen with emendations by Dr Johnson." James Boswell to William Johnson Temple (1775)

SATURDAY 4

1787 Burns met Clarinda (Mrs McLehose), in Edinburgh. His farewell song 'Ae Fond Kiss' was considered "the essence of a thousand love tales".

SUNDAY 5

"The meanest of mankind has considerable power to do good, and more to hurt himself and others." Thomas Reid, *Essays on the Active Powers of Man* (1785)

6 MONDAY

1799 Joseph Black died at home in his chair. Adam Smith once said of him, "No man has less nonsense in his head."

7 TUESDAY

1786 James Dalrymple of Orangefield introduced Robert Burns at a meeting of the Canongate Kilwinning Lodge in Edinburgh.

8 WEDNESDAY

1776 Princess Dashkova took up residence in Edinburgh's New Town with her son and daughter. The princess was well acquainted with the literati of the city.

1786 "I think I may safely pronounce him a genius of no ordinary rank." Prophetic words about Robert Burns from editor Henry Mackenzie in the newly launched *Lounger* magazine in Edinburgh.

1728 John Clerk of Eldin, artist and brother-in-law of Robert Adam, was born in Penicuik. In Scott's *Guy Mannering*, Clerk's table is described as "an emblematical chaos of literature and science".

1781 Sir David Brewster (d.1868) was born in Jedburgh. The much-honoured physicist invented many important optical devices but is best known for inventing the kaleidoscope.

1731 Erasmus Darwin (d.1802), physician, poet and natural philosopher was born. His son, Robert, and grandson, Charles, followed him to Edinburgh as medical students.

December 2010

13 MONDAY

1784 Samuel Johnson died. He expired "a little before seven in the evening, without a pang, though long oppressed with a complication of dreadful maladies, the great and good Dr Johnson, the pride of English literature and of human nature." *The Gentleman's Magazine*

14 TUESDAY

1756 John Home's *Douglas* was first performed at West Digges Theatre in the Canongate, Edinburgh. According to Alexander Carlyle, it "had unbounded success for a great many nights in Edinburgh and was attended by all the literati and most of the judges". On the same date in 1788 The Medical Society of Edinburgh received its Royal Charter from George III.

15 WEDNESDAY

Like his grandson Charles, Erasmus Darwin had ideas on evolution: "Organic life beneath the shoreless waves / Was born and nurs'd in oceans pearly caves."

THURSDAY *16*

1773 The biggest Tea Party in history took place in Boston.

FRIDAY *17*

1745 James Tytler (d.1804), surgeon, balloonist, writer and hapless entrepreneur was born at Fearn. He spent seven years editing the second edition of the *Encyclopedia Britannica* for a paltry 16 shillings a week.

SATURDAY *18*

1825 Sir Walter Scott's publisher, James Ballantyne, made a sombre call at 39 Castle Street to advise the author of serious financial problems.

SUNDAY *19*

1776 Thomas Paine published his first American Crisis essay with the famous line, "These are the times that try men's souls."

December 2010

20 MONDAY

1734 Dr Cumming presented, *On the signs, causes and Methods of Cure, of the Rabies Canina* to a group of medical students. The group was later constituted as the Medical Society of Edinburgh.

21 TUESDAY

1835 The politician and agriculturalist, Sir John Sinclair (b.1754) died aged 82. He compiled the *First Statistical Account of Scotland*, published in 1790.

22 WEDNESDAY

"The spirit of self-help is the root of all genuine growth in the individual." Samuel Smiles

1812 Samuel Smiles (d.1904), author of *Self-Help* and *Lives of Engineers* was born in Haddington near Edinburgh.

1745 Benjamin Rush (d.1813), signatory of the Declaration of Independence and a medical graduate of Edinburgh University, was born near Philadelphia. Of Scotland's capital he recounted, "My halcyon days have been spent in Edinburgh."

1776 2,400 men crossed the Delaware River with George Washington, a move that would prove a major victory in helping the American colonies to overthrow British government.

1774 Thomas Graham of Balgowan married Mary Cathcart, best known as *The Honourable Mrs Graham* in the portrait by Gainsborough exhibited at the Royal Academy in 1777.

December 2010

27 **MONDAY**
Public Holiday (UK)

1782 The Scots lawyer, philosopher and author of *The Elements of Criticism*, Henry Home (b.1696), Lord Kames, died in Edinburgh.

28 **TUESDAY**
Public Holiday (UK)

"No man ever did a designed injury to another, but at the same time he did a greater to himself."
Lord Kames

29 **WEDNESDAY**

1766 Charles Mackintosh, the chemist, was born. He amassed a fortune from a patent he obtained in 1823 detailing a process for waterproofing fabric that had been developed originally by the eminent surgeon, James Syme, while a student in Edinburgh.

THURSDAY *30*

1786 "The town is at present agog with the ploughman poet, who received adulation with native dignity," wrote Mrs Alison Cockburn to a friend, referring to the presence of Robert Burns in Edinburgh.

FRIDAY *31*

"That Action is best which procures the greatest Happiness for the greatest Numbers; and that worst, which, in like manner, occasions misery." Francis Hutcheson, *An Inquiry into the Original of our Ideas of Beauty and Virtue* (1725)

SATURDAY *1*
New Year's Day

1816 "On this day a new era opens to our view." Robert Owen, social and educational reformer, at the opening of the Institute for the Formation of Character in New Lanark

SUNDAY *2*

"The genius of philosophy, if carefully cultivated by several, must gradually diffuse itself throughout the whole society, and bestow a similar correctness on every art and calling." David Hume

January 2011

3 MONDAY
Public Holiday (UK)

"One of the most distinguished privileges which Providence has conferred upon mankind, is the power of communicating their thoughts to one another. Destitute of this power, reason would be a solitary and, in some measure, an unavailable principle." Hugh Blair

4 TUESDAY
Public Holiday (SCO)

"Beauty is no quality in things themselves. It exists merely in the mind which contemplates them." David Hume

5 WEDNESDAY

Of Alexander Carlyle, D.D. of Inveresk, *Kay's Portraits* records: "His talents as a preacher were of the highest order, and contributed much to introduce into the Scottish pulpit an elegance of manner and delicacy of taste, to which this part of the United Kingdom had been formerly a stranger, but of which it has since afforded some brilliant examples."

A Whim - or a visit to the Mud Bridge

The Lawnmarket Coach or A Journey Along The Mound (1786)

In the 1780s several citizens of Edinburgh were keen to have more direct access from the Old Town to the New Town and so opened a subscription to build a new thoroughfare. Subscribers of ten shillings were entitled to express their opinions, but those of five were only entitled to vote. In the end The Mound linking the Old and New Towns was built by other means and the subscribers then planned a celebratory ride over the new Mud Brig. When the Treasurer absconded with the funds however, the elaborate scheme had to be abandoned. Here Kay gives a rendition of an event that never happened. Noteworthy in the motley band of merchants and ladies is the coachman, George Boyd, a clothier who took a special interest in the creation of The Mound and the inscription on the post 'G.B.'s Bridge' is an allusion to this.

LAST SITTING of the OLD COURT of SESSION 11 of JULY 1808

·I·KAY· 1808·

Last Sitting of the Old Court of Session on 11th of July 1808 (1808)

The fifteen Lords are shown seated at one bench. Thereafter, by an Act of George III, the court was separated into Two Divisions which first assembled on 12th November 1808. Describing a semicircle from left to right they are: Lord Hermand, Lord Balmuto, Lord Bannatyne, Lord Armadale, Lord Cullen, Lord Polkemmet, Lord Hope, Sir Islay Campbell, Lord Dunsinnan, Lord Craig, Lord Glenlee, Lord Meadowbank Snr., Lord Woodhouselee, Lord Robertson and Lord Newton.

(*opposite top*) **David Smyth, Lord Methven (1799)**

(*middle*) **Sir William Miller of Glenlee Bt, Lord Glenlee (1799)**

(*lower*) **Sir William Macleod-Bannatyne, Lord Bannatyne (1799)**

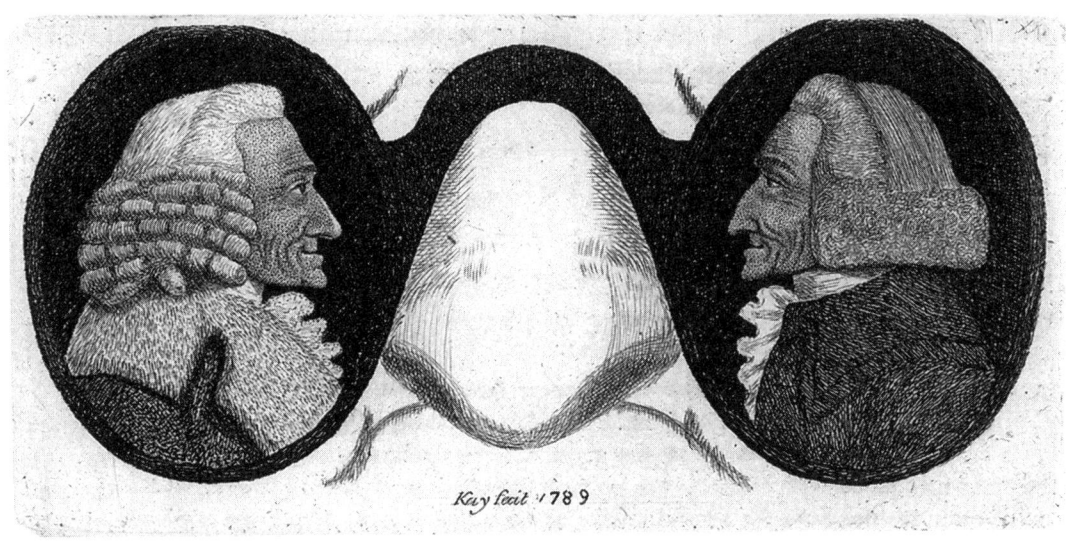

Voltaire, the French Philosopher and Mr Watson, an Edinburgh Messenger (1789)
The humble Mr Watson was deemed to bear a perfect resemblance to François-Marie Arouet,
otherwise known as the great philosopher Voltaire.

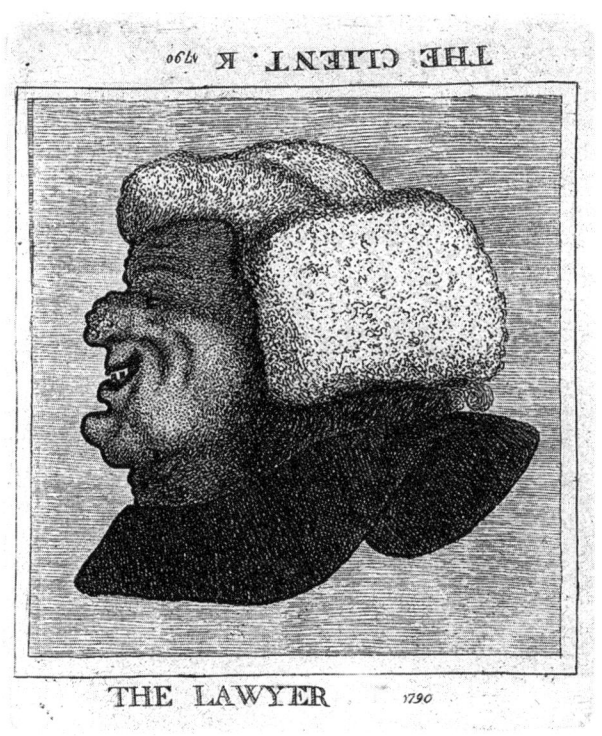

The Lawyer, The Client (1790) One of Kay's humorous topsy-turvy portraits.